Ready, Set, Go!

Ready, Set, Go!

Salon Business

How to Manage a Salon in Good Times and Bad

Jeff Grissler

2014

Ready, Set, Go! Salon Business: How to Manage a Salon in Good Times and Bad

Published in the U.S. by Ready, Set, Go! Publishing, LLC
215 Pascal Street
Fort Collins, Colorado 80524

Interior by Lee Cannon
Cover by Robin Krauss of Linden Design

ISBN 978-0-9911584-3-0

About the Author

Jeff Grissler has been where you are and understands the inner workings of the salon industry. As a business owner, he understands the business landscape. Jeff is a partner of, and the National Sales Manager for, Quest Resources—one of the salon industry's leading financing companies for furniture and equipment. His career in finance began on Wall Street and he has been involved in the multi-million dollar beauty industry for over twenty years. Jeff has financed over fifteen thousand salons, helping them open their doors or complete their remodeling projects through creative financing strategies.

It takes an experienced business owner like Jeff, who has run businesses large and small, to establish himself as a leader in cosmetology business education. Jeff has been in the trenches and truly understands what it takes to navigate the waters of business ownership, whether choppy or calm. He knows firsthand that business battles are won through planning, learning, taking chances, and a bit of good luck.

A gifted businessman and consultant, Jeff prides himself on his networking ability in bringing people together to share new ideas and explore partnerships. Through his skilled negotiations, he has convinced the banking industry to lift restrictions on the beauty industry. He has also negotiated contracts and leases with salon owners, spa owners, distributors, manufacturers, and banking management. Jeff Grissler can also mentor you, through the good times and bad. Reach out to him at jgrissler@questrs.com.

Jeff was born in New York City, then moved to the Jersey Shore. He was a New York City fireman for more than fifteen years and served during 9/11. Jeff now resides in Wilmington, North Carolina, with his wife, Coleen, and their three children, Kaytlyn, JT, and Julianna Rose.

Acknowledgments

I am so grateful to all the hundreds of wonderful people in the cosmetology industry who have shared their time, talents, and amazing stories with me through the years. Traveling for business can be lonely sometimes, but everywhere I've been, new friends have welcomed me. I want to thank the many people I've had the pleasure of meeting at beauty trade shows, industry events, sales meetings, and continuing-education classes.

Plenty of nights and weekends I missed being with family and friends because of business trips. When I got home, they were always there to greet me with open arms. The *Ready, Set, Go!* books exist without their support and encouragement. Thank you so much, you beautiful people!

Other Books from Ready, Set, Go! Publishing

The Start-Up Guide for Opening, Remodeling, and Running a Successful Beauty Salon

A Salon Owner's Guide to Wealth

The Salon Building Bible

The Modern Salon in Pictures

How to Offer 5-Star Service at Your Salon and Make Big Money!

The Start-Up Guide for Opening, Remodeling, and Running a Successful Barbershop

Barbershop Now!

Cosmetology School Graduate 1: All About Business

Cosmetology School Graduate 2: Life Lessons

Cosmetology School Graduate 3: How to Get a J.O.B. in a Salon

Salon and Booth Rental Employee Handbook

Table of Contents

Part One

How to Succeed
as a
Salon Manager

1

To Be a Great Salon, You Need a Strong Leader

How many of us have had jobs that never really taught us anything? We showed up every day and did what we had to do, not really enjoying it, just going through the motions. Maybe there was no one there who was like us, no one we could talk to who would understand us. Many of us long for that special person who will not only guide us, but also mentor us, spark our creativity, and enable us to grow as individuals. Or maybe you were one of the lucky ones and had people like that in your work life. I know I did and those guys helped me more than I can say!

When you opened your salon or became a salon manager, maybe leading a team wasn't even a thing you considered. Yes, you knew there would be responsibility, but a leadership role was not on your radar. You might not have anticipated being the person others come to for mentoring! When you did the unimaginable and opened the salon, suddenly you realized your life had changed. With that change came an enormous responsibility, not only to yourself but to the people you hired and oversee.

Every day, these people come to you looking for guidance and help. You've morphed not only into a leader, but also a psychologist, mother, father, and—more than one time—a shoulder to cry on. How you react to these situations separates you from other business owners. A true leader knows the way, goes the way, and shows the way. No matter what the situation, a true leader steadies the ship and stays on course.

Leadership Lessons—In the beauty salon there will be many times your stylists may make mistakes. Some will be really bad, others not so bad, but still things just didn't turn out right. As the leader, you must give the bad news or criticism. Not saying anything doesn't change the way things are done. They just continue and things won't get fixed. This approach doesn't do anything good for you as the owner or manager or for the stylists who answer to you. If you have honest feedback, share that with them in a positive and supporting way. That's the only way you can contribute anything to these people's lives and growth. How will they learn unless they see the way each issue is resolved?

Treating Everyone as Equals—There are many personalities in the salon. The ages, backgrounds, and viewpoints of the stylists will vary. One thing is for sure, though, every stylist will be watching how you handle problems within your team closely. Like a good captain of a ship, you must learn to treat everyone fairly. You have to be honest, transparent, and careful to treat everyone as equals. If a problem does arise, you must respond using the same approach every time. Each problem may be different, but how you handle the overall situation must stay the same. Playing favorites with your staff and treating people differently is a huge mistake.

Discipline Is Essential—We have all heard the expression that time is money, so we try to use time wisely. But it's also true that it always seems like you just don't have enough time to get everything done. The temptation is to tell yourself there's always tomorrow and you can finish everything then, but tomorrow always brings a new load of work!

Well, in order to be a great leader you need to be disciplined about time management. Start by writing things down. If you have a task list with ten items, cross them off as you get them done. Put the items that are most important first and work your way through the list. Proper time management will change your life. Write it all down, take care of each item, and follow through! Set this good example for your staff and encourage them to improve their time-management skills along with you. If it truly looks like a team effort to manage time, with everyone pitching in, then you'll see much more buy-in among your employees.

Make Them Believe—In order to get everyone on board and inspire them to follow you, your team must believe in you. Your values, how you treat people, what you wear to work, and your approach to problem solving will all be part of your leadership role. If you expect your team to come to work on time, dressed to the nines with the newest fashions, hair and nails perfect, then you the leader can't show up late for your first hair appointment wearing jeans, a t-shirt, flip-flops, with no make-up on, looking like you just rolled out of bed. Not a good example and certainly not a true leader.

Open Book—It's essential to have team meetings and include the entire staff. Having the meetings after work or on a day off assures that no one is rushing off to their next appointment, everyone is relaxed, and paying attention will be the most productive option. Everyone should be able to openly discuss issues and problems in the salon. This facilitates an open forum to share issues and eliminate the drama that arises in salons daily. This is what I call the open book strategy, because every person makes him/herself open and readable to others.

You will lead the discussion and make sure everyone feels able to discuss what's on their minds without interruptions. Each team member should have a few minutes to give input and openly discuss education, problems, procedures, and what may be bothering them. As a leader, it's crucial to not discount anything that's said, even if it's from the youngest employee. Remember, the youth of your salon will someday mentor others. Show them how to listen by listening yourself.

Also, these team meetings are a chance to show your employees how to treat each other in a drama-free way. Picture this, a young employee voices a problem during the meeting and you immediately rush to defend yourself, or whoever. What kind of message does that send? Here's the uncomfortable reality: The more defensive you are, the less your employees will trust your ability to handle feedback. They'll clam up and start trying to solve problems their way, behind your back!

However, a positive process for meetings will lead to positive feedback, changes in procedures, enhanced policies, and a better environment within the salon. The open book strategy will help the staff who feel intimidated when discussing disputes. Over time, your employees will feel closer to one another, work together better, and respect you more for having these team gatherings.

2

Management Goals of Your Salon

All business owners and managers face the challenge, regardless of the size of their salon, to inspire their staff to become the best they can, every day they come to work. The culture managers want to foster should be a primary consideration and is a daily challenge they all must work hard to meet. Deciding what drivers to put in place to have a positive impact is always tricky. What works and what doesn't usually becomes clear through old-fashioned trial and error. The key is to identify the drivers that your salon's employees accept, then use those drivers to encourage them to do their best work, innovate, and develop their creativity, while they also get along with and show respect for the salon owner, managers, and each other.

One of your most important tasks as the manager is to boil down a salon's many priorities and strategies into a simple plan, so that employees can remember it, internalize it, and act on it. With clear goals and metrics, everyone can push in the same direction, seeing clearly how their work contributes to the goals of the entire salon.

Rules of the Road—Maintaining a positive salon environment and keeping your employees happy is a constant battle. You want to create an environment where people want to be at work. Hanging a sign in the salon's employee break room with the policies will not be enough.

Incorporating the salon's rules of the road into team meetings and education is one strategy to use. Remind employees, often and thoughtfully, of the salon's vision and how the policies further that vision. Employees will eventually internalize these guidelines for behavior because you will help them see how the policies benefit them. With good guidelines, employees can concentrate on the work at hand, rather than on navigating the stressful politics, customer relations issues, and the daily drama problems that can plague a salon.

Team Players—Employees generally want to be part of a greater purpose that makes them feel like part of a larger whole. Everyone wants to belong to something; it's your role to make employees feel like your salon team is the best thing to belong to. Your employees will want to be on that team, in that club, because they believe in something. This cohesive attitude can be contagious if you model it yourself by treating employees as critical members of the team, by praising and reinforcing their efforts consistently, and by reminding employees of the salon's vision and how their hard work and observance of the guidelines in the employee rule book makes them fit into that vision.

Set Goals—Having a team of strike-out pitchers and home-run hitters would be ideal for your salon, but it's highly unlikely. The best you can expect is for employees to have home-run days and maybe even home-run weeks. You will have stylists and employees at many different levels. Their understanding of their roles and capabilities is a must. So is making them accountable for their daily, weekly, and monthly goals.

Make it one of your focuses to get your employees invested, so they care more about their duties and their position in your salon. If they become fully invested, they will understand their role and have a better feeling about your salon's systems and rules, and what they are capable of earning and achieving on a regular basis. Soon, they'll *want* to come to work and perform better each and every day.

The only way you can achieve this is by clearly defining and measuring each employee's goals. Then you must make sure that each department of the salon, if separate, will support the goals of the entire salon.

Once you get this system in place and running well, you will see the change. Your employees will feel motivated to get the job done, not just put in time behind the chair to collect a paycheck.

Develop Values—How you set the salon's values will probably come from the values you've been taught and have had instilled in you. Other managers, if your salon has them, in turn have to follow what you have taught and expressed to them. This ethic will move through them down to your employees. The critical part of this equation is *you* must be a mature person and treat people well. Being a bossy boss and upbraiding a stylist because he or she made a mistake is not a way to win influence on your salon's staff.

Values usually come from the top, but can be developed with input from everyone in the company. Holding company meetings will enable everyone give their opinions and assist with coming up with a good company value system.

What truly matters is that the company lives by the values you put in place, so reinforce them every day and don't tolerate behavior that's at odds with them.

The minute your employees start to see a disconnect between the stated values and how people are allowed to behave, the entire system of developing values will crumble, damaging the entire organization and sending the salon spiraling into the abyss of drama! Do I sound overly dramatic myself? Well, try it and see. Show your employees you allow violations of the stated values, and soon you won't *have* employees, or a company at all.

We've heard one bad apple can spoil the bunch. This is so true in the salon environment. One bad person can topple even the greatest salon. The key is to retrain or—worst-case scenario—get rid of this person when you see the problem starting. Cynicism is the first cancer cell, so to speak, that can metastasize within a salon, when that first employee starts to feel the company is not actually living out its core values.

If the salon has problems—and it will—the key to positive management is to have clear discussions with everyone about how to handle issues respectfully with each other. When you have problems with gossip, disrespectfulness among coworkers, lateness, whatever may arise, they must be dealt with immediately. Your quick action will make every employee understand the salon's culture is real and is based on respect, and that your salon's rules are equally real. The result will be a comfort level among your employees and a true feeling of safety within your salon.

3

Why Your Salon Needs Rules

Think back to when you were a child: Your parents or guardians established rules for you to follow and (maybe more, maybe less) enforced them. Clean up your room, come home directly from school, do your homework before supper, fold your clothes, make your bed. No matter what the rule, you basically learned you were expected to follow instructions, and life at home was simple and non-problematic as long as the rules were followed. When the rules were honored, the grown-ups were happy, things ran smoothly, life was good.

Fast forward to your work life and your salon environment. Let's look at your salon as a family unit, a household. Your employees are members of the household, who need basic rules to make things run smoothly, establish relationships, and make living in the house harmonious for all.

This isn't easy, but it *can* be accomplished. You as the leader must provide an environment that makes understanding your salon's core principles easy through simple rules. The first step is make those rules and ensure every employee understands them. Establish that employees are expected to follow the rules. If the rules are not followed, there will be ramifications.

As an employer you will also be expected to keep score with your employees who don't follow the rules. Setting standards brings people together, harmonizing the group as one, and aligns them with each other through a common set of guidelines that everyone knows and understands don't have space for exceptions. The goal here is simple: rules keep the team members in check, everyone is happy, life in the salon is good.

Let's look at a salon with no rules in place. If you don't give people metrics, smart people will quickly make up their own. In fact, there's a lot of behavioral psychology research around the fact that, the fewer rules in place, the quicker others will step in for you and make up their own rules. They may even think they're doing you a favor. These people are usually the strongest of the group. In many cases, this dynamic tends to divide the salon and causes…dare I say it?… DRAMA, the demise of many salons. Put simply: No rules equals drama, which directly equals unhappy employees and unsatisfied customers. This leads to the slow death of any salon through employee walkouts, client loss, and a salon environment that's toxic and unfit to work in.

We have identified that the salon needs rules. Now, these rules need to be written into an employee handbook. Each employee should be given a salon employee handbook outlining the rules you've put in place. Give the handbook to them right when they start working for your salon.

Review the employee handbook with every employee, so each

understands your salon's rules, consequences of breaking the rules, and what is expected from them as employees of your business. The employee will then sign the employee handbook and keep a copy, and you, as the salon owner or manager, will keep the original on file.

If you already have a team but have never had an employee handbook, use a team meeting time to introduce a new employee handbook, explain what's inside, and announce the policy that all current employees need to sign it, just the same as any new employees hired in the future.

Basic Rules for Salon Employees

- Come to the salon on time and fully prepared for work.
- No alcohol or drug use at work.
- Keep your work space and the common space neat and clean.
- Leave the drama at home.
- Treat employees/coworkers in a professional manner.
- If you're sick, stay home.
- Notify manager or owner as soon as possible when you need to call in sick.
- Keep your appearance clean cut and professional.
- No cellphone use is allowed at your styling station.
- Flip flops are for the beach, not work.
- Personal hygiene is critical in the salon environment.
- Clean the dispensary after every use.
- If you need to borrow from a coworker, ask first, then give the item back afterward.
- Theft in the salon will not be tolerated. Borrowing without permission is theft.
- Greet each customer by name.

- Always say "thank you" to your client.
- Work time is for focusing on clients.
- Recommending products is part of your job description.
- Keep eye contact and body language professional.
- Keep physical contact appropriate and professional.
- Never get defensive with clients; the customer is always right. Instead, listen for the lesson in clients' complaints.
- Team meetings and advanced education in the salon are part of your job. Show up and participate, because your opinion counts.

4

Knowing Your Salon's Heartbeat

No two employees are alike. From attitude to work ethic to skills and abilities, all workforces are made up of individuals, each with their own unique set of values and priorities. Whether it's money, time off, recognition, or praise, your employees have a driving force that pushes them to achieve. As a leader and the manager of the salon, it's your responsibility to know what motivates your team.

An important first step to discovering what makes your employees tick is understanding motivation itself. It's a subject that's been studied extensively throughout time and there is a wide variety of theories that attempt to explain why we, as humans, do the things we do. It's critical to your success at leading to understand what motivates your own employees. The key is to understand your company's heartbeat.

There are many steps to take to achieve a common goal of unity in the salon. Each phase of leadership will play a role in obtaining one common heartbeat with your team. This isn't something that will happen overnight; all good things take time to build. Let's take a look at some key leadership techniques that will help you achieve your goals.

Show You Care—People who inspire get the best out of their employees. Like a good coach who inspires his team to strive for victory, you as the salon owner must show you care and want the best for your employees. Showing you care for an employee as an individual, not just as a worker, creates a level of trust and compassion that makes a big impression on employees and clients alike.

Hold Team Meetings—Team meetings are a key to gaining and maintaining a true understanding of what is going on in your salon and how people feel about you, their peers, the products you sell, the salon's vibe, and anything else pertaining to the business.

A great way to open meetings is by giving your team members a chance to air their problems or ask their questions anonymously. The week before your meeting, invite your team to write their questions or concerns down and put them in a closed box, or email them directly to you. At the meeting itself, read out and discuss the problems and questions. Go through and address every one as thoroughly as you can, without skipping.

Keeping things anonymous leaves the day-to-day drama in the box and lets your team truly express what's on their minds. It means your employees won't feel put on the spot. Anonymity also prevents any hard feelings, in case someone is trying to address an issue with a coworker. Do this once a month.

Explain Your Vision—Show your team and explain that coming to work is not just about getting a paycheck. Yes, that's important and you want your employees to do well financially, but it's up to you to show your team the vision of the salon. You want them to be inspired, creative, and feel pride because they work in a place that's different from the other salons in your area. Allowing them to show their creativity and express themselves creates something that's just as important to them as it is to you. This will help your team members internalize what the salon is trying to accomplish.

Promote Product Knowledge—Your staff must use the products you sell. If they don't, they haven't bought into your system. Your body can't function without a heart. The heart of the salon is the systems and products you sell and use in your back bar. If employees don't use or understand what you sell in your salon, then you can't possibly be working efficiently. Product knowledge is essential to your salon's success. Why would your customers buy from you unless you have proper knowledge of the products and systems you have in place?

Education is essential. It's a great idea to have your product salespeople organize classes or have your team attend beauty trade shows, so they can see new styles, cuts, techniques, and products in person that enhance what you do on a daily basis.

Emphasize Customer Service—Treat people how you like to be treated, then multiply that by two. People enjoy being treated like kings and queens; it's not out of style. Explain to your staff how you want them to treat clients. Take your team to an expensive restaurant and have them observe the level of customer service. You can't expect your staff to give five-star service if they haven't experienced it themselves. Educate them, explain to them, and always treat them with respect. If you are giving people of all levels five-star treatment yourself, the five-star mentality will flow down to your employees and then to your customers.

Owning a salon is not easy and getting a full grasp of the heartbeat of your salon will take time. This task is not one to set aside for when you "have more time" or aren't "in the busy season" anymore. You must work on it daily.

Keeping the passion for the art of cosmetology alive is what motivates salon employees. Groups of people, from whole societies to the smallest salon teams, achieve great things when their hearts beat as one.

5

Relationships at Work

The salon is a melting pot of many different personalities, set to simmer in an environment that can become really high pressured.

Your group of salon or spa employees is working hard at keeping clients looking handsome or beautiful. The effort that takes on any given day can be overwhelming. Standing on your feet coloring or cutting hair, giving massages or facials, is not easy. It's not shocking that tensions may grow, personalities may conflict, and we may think we can set aside rules just to get things done, but how we each conduct ourselves and deal with that in the salon is extremely important to the success of the business.

When the salon is busy, it's not uncommon for temperatures to rise. I'm sure you can think of examples of rude behavior in the workplace, including colleagues making petty comments, communicating in an abrasive manner, even screaming at one another, backbiting, or simply expecting that people will do things for them at a whim, without a "please" or "thank you." We've all seen it and have done it ourselves, but the salon or spa is not the place for it, nor will colleagues put up with it for long.

Many people seem to think because they are so busy and stressed, they are allowed to be unpleasant to their colleagues, or show up late to things without apologizing.

Some see incivility as a lack of good breeding. Others have even told me they think incivility is a sign of weakness. Whatever the reason, there is no excuse for treating people with a lack of respect or showing just plain bad manners at work.

Why is civility on the job such an important issue? Incivility reflects poorly on the workplace. It sends a message to customers about the salon or spa and is related to increased consumer complaints. It also affects employee loyalty—why would your talented people want to stay, when rudeness is the norm? A lack of civility also drains productivity because employees are spending time and emotional energy on dealing with stress.

To be successful, there needs to be one rule in the salon or spa in regards to getting along and acting professional to one another: All will get along; those who don't will be terminated.

The salon as an organization needs to take on the responsibility of managing interpersonal relationships, so interactions among employees, managers, and clients remain positive and respectful. When the salon's leaders truly lead, they create a positive atmosphere, built on the highest expectations of professionalism, not just when convenient, not just when time permits, but all the time, every time.

6

Why You Need a Mentor, Even When You're the Manager

When you opened your salon, you may have had no idea how much of an impact you would have on the people who work for you. Your salon's culture, the values you instill, and the work ethic you portray all have an effect on everyone around you. When you had visions of opening your salon, you knew you would have the responsibilities of employees, payroll, rent, insurance, and marketing your business. What you didn't realize is you would become a mentor, teacher, parent, and sometimes babysitter to your entire salon team.

There will be times when Murphy's Law strikes your salon from every which way. Employees coming in late, a drama-filled episode between your stylist and your front desk person, an unhappy customer who blamed her bad color on one of your best stylists, a walk out from two of your up-and-coming colorists, and a landlord who will not fix your leaky roof. All eyes will be on you when these situations arise and how you handle each will be the basis of your teaching process. Your staff members—or should I call them pupils—will observe your every move. Their minds, like sponges sucking up water, will be ingesting every movement, every word you say, and every emotion you show while handling these very chaotic situations.

The techniques you use to handle these situations may come from your parents, former teachers, and salon owners you have worked for before. Ideally, the people you learned from were able to instill good personal and business ethics in you, which you can pass on to your own staff now.

You may not have known it, but the leaders in your life undoubtedly mentored you. That mentoring enabled you to do well in your career, create opportunities for yourself, and now own a salon. Since your career has blossomed, it's the perfect time in your life to mentor back. Help your salon team develop their career paths by learning from you, which will help them earn more and have a fuller life.

What Is Mentoring?

Mentors are experienced, trusted advisors or counsellors who have successful careers and proven track records. As a mentor, you make a commitment to support and encourage your mentees (salon employees) as they pursue their career goals. Mentors are not usually paid for their services. Your compensation is watching your salon staff members blossom into successful individuals.

Mentors:

- Encourage their mentees to develop careers that reflect their skills, potential and goals, simply put, and make them the best they can be at whatever they do.
- Offer wisdom, knowledge, experience, constructive criticism, connections, and resources.
- Focus on the mentee's overall career direction rather than on day-to-day concerns.
- Set an example for the level of professional conduct and success their mentees hope to achieve.

Why Mentor?

People become mentors for a variety of reasons. You may have benefited from a relationship with a mentor and want to pass that benefit on to others, to give back to your organization, industry or community, to build a reputation for developing new talent, or you value the perspective you gain by seeing yourself, your profession, and your career through your mentee's eyes.

Mentoring can help you stay current, re-energize yourself professionally, and expand your network in new directions. Look at it this way: You're in the salon every day; why not mentor your way through each day? What more can your employees ask for? The results will not only be significant, but the payback will be worth its weight in gold.

7

How to Keep Your Money in Your Wallet and Out of the Drain

What could be more discouraging than to work all year; pay your employees, your landlord, your suppliers, your utilities, and everything else; and then realize you neglected to pay yourself? Yet, that's exactly what most salon owners are doing when they ignore several simple disciplines that can easily turn a break-even business profitable.

The current numbers in the cosmetology industry indicate 80% of salons are losing money, 15% are breaking even, and only 5% are turning a profit.

Let's look at the 80% that are losing money, here is what I've seen happening, time and time again: The salon owner is working behind the chair, doing what he or she loves to do. The owner certainly deserves an income for the top-notch services he or she offers, however, the lion's share of that well-deserved income goes toward paying the expenses in the salon, instead of into the owner's pocket.

Obviously, these owners would be financially better off working in someone else's salon, focusing on their art, but it doesn't have to be that way. Here are three simple strategies you can implement today that will have a dramatic influence on gaining back your personal income and moving your salon into profitability:

1. Look at Lowering Expenses—Your expense sheet should be the first place you look for more money, rather than trying to increase revenue. Why? Because every dollar you cut in expenses can go directly to paying other expenses, while every dollar of increased revenue produces only a small fraction of profit.

Think about it this way: If you are an owner working behind the chair in your salon and part of your personal income is going to pay expenses in your salon, every dollar you trim in expenses will be like a pay raise. On the flip side, each dollar you spend over budget will be like a pay cut to you!

The impact of lowering costs by just $100: If you are blessed with a 10% profit margin in your business and you wanted an additional $100 in profit this month, you would have to generate an additional $1,000 in revenue or approximately an additional 15 hours of billable time, based on industry averages. If you can cut $100 in expenses this month by taking 15 minutes to look at certain expense areas, you accomplish the same thing. And the recurring expense cuts accrue to the bottom line month after month.

Where should you look to cut expenses? Cutting the take-home pay of salon employees is pretty much out of the question, since they can likely take their skills elsewhere if they're not paid fairly. While this is your largest expense, it's also the most difficult to cut. The second and third largest expenses for most salons are also difficult to cut because they're rent and inventory, which covers the retail you sell as well as the products you use at the point of service.

It's possible to save costs by keeping less inventory on hand. However, without adequate inventory, you are giving up sales opportunities. Rent is generally fixed over a long-term lease or financing plan, so there's rarely an chance to cut costs there. You could open a small window of opportunity when your lease is coming due for renewal, because you have the bargaining chip of signing a longer lease if the landlord will give you a break on rent, or will even agree not to raise the rent for a certain period.

The problem with asking for a longer lease in exchange for lower or fixed rent is the uncertainty involved. Neither you nor the landlord knows if your business will survive for three years, or even three more months, so you need ot be prepared to show evidence your business is healthy before your landlord will even consider a rent deal. Still, it never hurts to ask! More on this in Chapter 36.

If you have a mortgage on your salon space instead of a lease, refinancing could be an option, so start at your bank to get a little education on refinancing, then widen your search from there.

Next in the lineup of expenses are advertising costs and credit card processing fees, followed by the remainder of your indirect expenses. These are the areas of most potential for cutting costs! In fact, 2% redirected from waste to profit, over time can build up, generate interest, and turn into a substantial retirement account.

Advertising is crucial, no questions about it, but the range of methods of promoting your salon is much wider than you think. Why pay the cost of printing and mailing flyers when you can send e-notices of special deals in your salon? Facebook, Twitter, Tumblr, Pinterest, and blogs—and the list expands daily—are powerful low-cost or no-cost tools to get your message out to the community. The more hustle you have with alternative advertising methods, the more cash you'll save on traditional means.

Even though it's further down the list and carries a smaller price tag, the absolute best and easiest place to start lowering costs is with your credit card processing fees. There's a service out there called Integrity Payment Systems, evaluated and recommended by the L'Oreal Professional Product Division, that can generate a free cost analysis of credit card processing fees and hidden charges, to give you an evaluation of what you're paying, compared to what you should be paying, for processing.

Other products and services exist as well, so an hour searching the internet and comparing processing systems and possibilities could save you days of rooting around in the rest of your budget for ways to cut expenses. Even Costco offers affordable credit card processing systems to their warehouse members, so get creative with potential sources of better deals.

If you cut your processing costs by 25% or 50%, you could redirect as much as 1% of your total revenues straight to your bottom line. Taking a hard and close look at your expenses is the first step.

2. Set Up an Emergency Fund—Even if you are paying off a mortgage on your salon space or have credit card debt, just tell yourself it's mandatory to set up a pot of emergency money first. Unexpected expenses are part of life and without cash reserves, your salon is a big, fat sitting duck!

An emergency fund will keep you out of debt when surprise expenses crop up, which they will, trust me. Any financial planner will tell you this. The irony is, almost no one does it! It's really tough to envision the value of having money sitting around, when you see expenses piling up every day and your credit card balance growing and growing. But remember this: It's even tougher to watch the IRS pull money out of your business, completely taking away your choice in how that money is allocated, so avoid it!

Imagine your peace of mind, knowing you have enough cash in the bank to handle almost any emergency expense. Integrity Payment Systems also has a free service called AutoSave which will take a small percentage of every credit card transaction and move it to your savings account, automatically. Once you set up the program, a very small portion of every transaction—every day, every week, every year—will transfer into a cash account you designate. These reserves will grow faster than you realize.

3. Eliminate Debt—Paying the minimum on your credit cards each month is a guaranteed way to enrich the banks and keep you stuck on the credit card hamster wheel. How can you pay off those cards without increasing revenue? One way is to take advantage of Integrity Payment System's EasyPay system. It lets you designate a small portion of every credit card transaction in your salon to automatically transfer toward the principle on your debt. You still make your regular payments, and EasyPay will transfer a portion of each transaction to pay down the rest. Think how fast and painless paying debt with this system could be.

Start This Minute—Implementing these three simple strategies can make a dramatic difference in the level of satisfaction you get from your business. There are plenty of tools and apps on the market that can help you become one of the 5% of salon owners turning a profit each year. It's your money, be the master of it!

8

Customers Have Feelings Too

You could fill your salon with the most expensive equipment, hire the finest interior decorator to finish the interior, employ the best marketing guru in town, and build the best hair salon staff in the country, but none of these wise ideas will guarantee your clients will be happy. None of these methods directly make your clients feel important. Many of us lose track of the significance of remembering clients have feelings, too.

Every person in the world wants to feel important on any given day. We certainly remember when someone went out of their way to make us feel special or appreciated. It even could have been a very small gesture, but whatever it was, we'll remember, talk about it, and share the experience with friends and family. Most of us will go out of our way to be around that person or their place of business again.

People gravitate to those who make them feel special; that's a fact. Finding ways to use this phenomenon to benefit your business isn't brain surgery. Training your staff—and yourself—to perform services and interact with clients in ways that show appreciation, until it comes naturally, is a modest investment that produces huge returns. These practices of appreciation must start at your front desk and continue throughout the entire salon.

Use Your Client's Name—The easiest thing to do is to remember and use your client's name. Your receptionist knows the client is coming in at a certain time. The appointment is on his or her computer or logged in the appointment book. How nice is it when you walk into a place of business, to be greeted with, "Good morning, Ms. Smith, it's so nice to see you again and we're looking forward to your service today"?

Wow. Was that hard? No, of course not, but that's the first step. The second step is when the stylist and shampoo person greet the same client and use his or her name as well. This is a sample of an easy way to make someone feel extremely special. Did you do this in your salon today? You have their names, use them. These simple practices are such easy ways to make your clients feel special.

Acknowledge Each Client—We all have experienced waiting a really long time in line for something. Maybe it was sitting in a doctor's office. Has a doctor's office receptionist ever said sorry for making you wait? Most of the time, you go unnoticed and made to feel your time is not valuable. Well, *your* clients' time is valuable. They have jobs, families just like you, and I'm sure they have gone out of their way to make it to their appointment with you on time.

When your clients are sitting in the waiting area, acknowledge they're there. Walk over, smile, and say hello. Shake their hand, give them a hug. These small things diminish the fact that you may be running late, because you went out of your way to make them feel special and let them know they're important. Remember the doctor's office when you were ignored. You don't want to be that person; that should never happen in your salon.

Apologize—When in business, always expect the unexpected. Don't think your salon and staff will never run into problems. You have many different personalities, so the stage is already set for drama and stress, which can spill over into the client's experience. Add to that, chemicals, scissors, razors, electrical equipment, and water. Accidents are just waiting to happen all over the salon! You could start to wonder: How is it that more bad things don't occur in the salon in a given day?

Whatever the circumstances that do arise—whether you singe an ear with a curling iron, spatter hair dye on a face, or only slip and bump into your client—remember that the customer is always right and you ought to be the first to apologize. When things do go terribly wrong and Murphy's Law strikes, make sure you and your staff start off with a simple, "We are sorry." A "sorry" goes along way. This is a simple way to create a loyal customer. The better person always apologizes first; don't let your ego get in the way.

Listen—How many times has someone had to say, "Are you listening to me?" Maybe it was your children, spouse, or clients? Most people can tell when you're listening to them. It makes people feel important when you really give them your ear and pay attention to what they're saying. Especially when they're telling you how they want their hair! Beyond this, however, your client may be going through an illness, divorce, or work-related problem and really need to vent. Listening to their stories is important to them because true listening in today's world is rare. You have to stand right next to them as you cut or apply a hair color, so why not pay attention to what your client has to say? If it makes them feel good, go out of your way to be a good listener.

Training your salon team to become good listeners is just as important. They're representing *your* company. You want to make sure they are applying the exact color or giving the hair style your customer asks for. It's not always the extra stuff, the stories, your employees have to learn to listen to, but the service your client is requesting.

Make Them Part of Something—Making your clients part of your business is crucial. Sometimes it means you have to think out of the box to include them. If you have a blog or a Facebook page, ask your clients if you can "make them famous" and use their photos on the site, to show off their beautiful hair and great look. If your distributor is offering education to your staff, include some of your clients. Invite them come in for a free service and use them as models. This will make them feel special and also give them some bonding time with you and your staff.

If you are having a ladies' night out or bros' day, include some clients. Inviting them will make them feel special; they may not participate, but the invite will surely let them know they were wanted. Sometimes the thought is all the matters in making someone's day.

Thank You—The easiest way to make any customer feel good and appreciated is to say "thank you." It doesn't cost you a thing to show how much you appreciate that you have loyal clients, who keep coming back to your salon. How many times have you forgotten to say "thank you," when you had the perfect chance?

A good handshake or hug goes along way, too, if your clients have shown they are cool with hugs. A firm handshake communicates respect and liking just as loudly and clearly as your words of gratitude.

I told you in the beginning of this chapter that saying hello using the client's name is important. It's just as important to say goodbye and thank them using their name as well. It also makes a big impression when your staff does the same thing.

I always use a particular saying and it has worked for me for over twenty-five years. There isn't a day that goes by that I don't use this: "Thank you for your business. As always, it is well appreciated. Your continued business is appreciated by my family as well."

All of us should implement these practices at work each day. When you practice these simple routines, it will make your work more enjoyable and create a strong base of clients, who will continue to support your employees and your business.

9

What Is the Proper Business Greeting?

We have all been put in a position where someone comes over to say hello, leans in, and hugs you. Not just a light hug but a big, old bear hug. You try to get out of their grasp without offending them, but they just don't seem to let go. You are not sure how to react or what to do. Maybe you don't know this person well enough to hug back. Could be, you never met them before and even if you did, they didn't make a big enough impression on you to remember.

A simple smile or hello would have been more than enough. It's certainly an awkward moment when someone says hello or greets you this way. How will they feel if you don't hug back? You feel weird if you do and weird if you don't.

What's the proper protocol when you meet a client for the first or second time, when you greet them at the reception area or at your styling station? What if this person reaches in for the big hug, are you one of those stylists who throws up your hand and gives a high-five yelling, "Give me some love!" Or maybe you prefer to do a hip-check and give them a little love-tap? Do you lean in for a kiss? Is that how you would want to be greeted when someone says hello to you? There is proper protocol for everyone. You will have to use your judgment on which type of greeting you use when welcoming clients.

This is all part of the learning curve with customer service and sometimes the best judgment call is using good old fashion manners. If you are wondering if you should or shouldn't hug, kiss, or high-five, then don't. If someone is coming close to you to embrace you or give you a bear hug, step back and put out your hand for a handshake. This awkward greeting stage feels like minutes are passing when in reality it's only a few seconds, but your hand will signal the other person that the big hug is not appropriate.

Saying hello with a handshake is a big part of meeting someone for the first time. What is appropriate is also sometimes confusing. Yes, you should show that you are a friendly person and you are happy to meet this person for the first time, but remember, it's a client. This is not a blind date or a get-together with your BFFs or a class reunion with your old high school buddies. Each of these may and should have a different greeting practice. But we have to understand that everyone and each circumstance is different in terms of what is acceptable and what is not. Putting out your hand for a greeting, especially with clients, sets the tone for what is appropriate. This establishes the greeting so no one is caught in an awkward stage of not knowing what to do. Leave the hugs for later, if you both feel the need, when your client leaves the salon or spa.

In many cultures, hugging and even kissing are quite appropriate. How many times have you see people kiss on both sides of the cheeks. In the Parisian culture kisses are meant for close friends or relatives and may be acceptable with some but not all clients. Unless you're in Europe, the double-cheek kiss is a no-no. In America culture, some parts of the country do initiate a quick hug, which is much like the Parisian double-cheek kiss. This of course is reserved for someone you know. One should not hug or kiss someone they do not know or have met for the first time.

New Client Protocol

Handshake—The protocol and etiquette is that business begins and ends with a handshake, a firm hand-to-hand connection with two to three pumps. If you feel like you really need to give a strong hello, reach over with the opposite hand and put it on top of both you and your customer's hands, grasping both. This gives a sign of power and authority, that you are in touch with this person and will take charge from this point on. No need to squeeze the life out of their hand. Unless you're trying to show them you've been pumping weights at the gym every morning, make it a simple, even-pressured handshake.

A handshake is so versatile. It opens as an introduction, an acknowledgement, hello, goodbye, a well-done, and a great-to-see-you. The handshake is safe and warm, should never give the feeling that you are overdoing it by overwhelming someone with an inappropriate greeting. Not all people like physical contact so this provides an appropriate way to reach out and connect without encroaching on someone's personal space. A pat on the back may also be considered a little friendlier without breaking the business guidelines.

Hug—How can we tell if your client is open to a hug or prefers the handshake? In this case, it doesn't matter; put your hand out when you meet them. This will eliminate any embarrassing moments of both of you standing there looking at each other, wondering what to do. Tough call. However, as you get to know people, you will learn. We have learned in business that we need to treat our customers as unique. No two customers are the same. We need to identify their wants and expectations, then fulfill them. There are some clients who prefer a phone call to a text or email for an appointment reschedule or reminder. No different than the customer who prefers the big hug hello or nothing at all.

Knowing Your Customer—This is not groundbreaking advice. This is just simple knowledge that you will pick up with experience. As you grow into your position in the salon, you'll understand how each one of your coworkers, friends, and clients expect to be treated and greeted. This comes with age and time and is part of the learning curve. There will be customers you adore and some who are more difficult and will require you to take a few deep breaths before you communicate with them.

The ones you adore will most likely feel the same way about you and will want the big hello and hug. It's the other who will most likely accept the handshake or just a simple hello. It's up to you to get to know all your clients well enough, so that every time they see you, they're so happy to be in the salon with you they will *want* to give you a hug.

Saying Goodbye—In life, saying goodbye can be happy, sad, gratifying, or just plain, old, "Get me out of here; I can't wait to leave!" There will be different goodbyes with each of your clients. If the service didn't go as expected and the client is not happy, please remember you are a professional You're no longer in cosmetology school. Stamping your feet, screaming, cursing, and flipping your client the bird is not an appropriate way to end a bad service experience.

The salon industry is a very small industry and it will amaze you how your actions come back and haunt you, if you act inappropriately. Always remember the handshake and a simple good-bye is a professional way to end any meeting, whether it went well or poorly.

There always may be one exception to the rule, in the case when your client is so satisfied with a great hair cut or new style or color, they may feel the need for a hug, air-kiss, high-five, fist-bump, or just fell like doing an impromptu tango like you just won *Dancing with the Stars*, but only go along with it if that client initiates the happy ending!

10

The Lost Art of Thank-You Cards

Working in the salon business is not easy. Juggling family, relationships, personal affairs, your social life, and trying to keep clients happy is not only challenging, it's downright daunting. In general, as owners of salons or employees, we seem to cope. Life goes on, work continues, and we develop an equilibrium with the daily challenges the salon environment brings.

With the busy schedules we manage, sometimes the most important people in our professional lives get neglected: Clients! It's not that we take advantage of the relationships we've developed, but sometimes we simply forget to say thanks. Think about this, how many of us give a pat on the back or a quick thanks before a client climbs out of the styling chair? How often does your show of appreciation seemed whole-hearted? We have to remember, life as we know it would be drastically different without our clients.

How can we give our customers the recognition they deserve? There are plenty of ways to say thank you. Sure, with technology you can use a text, Tweet, Facebook, Instagram, or SnapChat to send a quick thanks to your customers. That would simply save time and get the job done; easy, right? The clients leave and they aren't even in their cars to drive away before you text them a thank you? That works. And, hey, that's shows you made the effort. Job done, right? Well, maybe, maybe not.

A text message is a lost cause; it just doesn't cut it. The simple reason is that a digital format doesn't convey emotion well enough for you to come across as meaning what you say. Somehow, when we get big, bold capital letters and thickets of exclamation points on the phone saying, "THANK UUUUU!!!!!!" it just isn't the same as opening a card from the mailbox and reading a handwritten note, is it?

Think back. Can you ever remember a time you saw your grandmother, or maybe your mom or dad, sitting at the kitchen table writing a thank-you card? The thank-you may have been for a birthday present, a dinner, a bouquet of flowers, anything. Probably it seemed old-fashioned and you wondered why they did it. Why the outdated communication mode?

I remember my mother making me write out thank-you cards to my aunts and uncles for coming to my graduation, sending me Christmas presents, all those events and special occasions. I hated even thinking about writing those notes and never really understood. Why was the process so important? For you, too, the thought of sitting down before or after work to write a thank-you to a client, just for coming in for a service, may seem like pure craziness.

The truth is, the boring stuff your parents made you do never actually goes out of fashion. Interestingly enough, recent studies of gratitude have found a statistical correlation of gratitude to increased optimism, reduced stress, and a better night's sleep. The added bonus is the clients you are sending the thank-yous to are ultimately extremely happy.

The few among us who sit down and actually write a bread-and-butter thank-you note are likely to be aware that, by doing so, they are not only on a trend, but also on their way to becoming happier and more social people. It is now being said that this good-mannered approach of thanking customers seems to be experiencing a moment of vogue.

Why is it all the rage again? Despite the incursions of electronic media, the handwritten note is alive and well. The fact is, your client knows you sat down and took the time to personally write something special. This small note to say thank you in business is a way to communicate a social affection. It's a bond of trust and dependence in a form of a simple card. This note re-emphasizes the personal relationship between you and that precious client, and shows you really do appreciate him or her. Your clients will recognize the effort you made on their behalf and will be more likely to reciprocate, in the form of visiting your salon more frequently and remaining a reliable customer for the long term.

11

Yes, Your Salon Needs Public Relations

Let's start simple. What in the world is Public Relations anyway? There are many different ways to interpret and define PR, but for argument's sake, Webster's Dictionary defines PR as "the business of inducing the public to have understanding for and goodwill towards a person, firm, or institution."

In short, PR is relating to your public, creating goodwill. And who doesn't need a little bit more goodwill these days, eh?

Some PR campaigns help with damage control, other PR strategies build networks and community partnerships, all with the hopes of being highlighted by the media to attract, keep, and strengthen the loyalty of existing customers.

Unlike marketing and advertising, PR takes advantage of unpaid communication channels, such as media outlets (i.e. social media, blogs, newspapers, etc.) and community relationships (your clients)—and when you're struggling to succeed, unpaid channels make even more sense to your bottom line. Keeping that in mind, here are three quick and easy PR tips:

Evaluate Your Reputation—Your reputation is everything. Take a step back and look at the mission of your business, or better yet your actual mission statement, if you have one. Reevaluate and identify characteristics you want to be known for. Create a list of crystal-clear key messages that positively communicate your business, products, and staff. Encourage your staff to broadcast these messages through their work. Live your brand out loud!

Ask Your Audience—How well do you know your clients? Really, how well? Do you know for certain how many clients come to you via your Facebook page or Web site, versus word-of-mouth referrals? Ask questions! It's amazing what you'll find out. Maybe no one is really reading those emails…so ASK why not. Maybe every one of your clients uses Twitter, maybe not—ASK! Maybe your top 5% of clients prefer direct mail offers, maybe not—ASK! Why spend a dime more if you aren't certain of your clients' needs and wants?

Find Communication Channels—Research community groups, Web sites, publications, and local and regional media sources that match your target markets. If you're targeting the older generations, then it's best to stick to traditional means of advertising, such as newspapers, newsletters, and direct mail. However, if your target market is younger, then there's a whole world of free or inexpensive ways to flex your PR muscle: Facebook, Twitter, Pinterest, Tumblr, a YouTube channel with videos of your stylists at work; the cloud is the limit these days!

Review social media sources and seek advice from PR professionals if you need direction on how to best communicate with your customers through the ever-changing world of social media.

Evaluate, ask, and communicate. Sure I make it sound simple, but true PR strategy takes time, energy, and due-diligence. Nothing happens overnight. Take time to really own and implement your strategy or find a trusted agency or PR consultant to help guide your brand to success.

How can working with a PR agent or agency quickly get your business back on track? Hello? Extra hands and minds on your business! The right PR agency will quickly become part of your brand, thinking and acting solely on how your business is communicated to your current client base and potential new clients. Although I'm the first to say good, solid PR efforts take time and energy, if you hand over the reigns to someone who has the time and expertise to focus on the communication strategy of your brand, your own time and energy can go into ensuring potential clients have an awesome product to enjoy, once they hear good things about your business and decide to come in.

Never reached out to the press? Allow your agent to take the driver's seat, finding the best media contacts and working on building your salon's story. Don't have enough time to dedicate to social media? A really skilled PR agent will find the right mix (and curate it!) for your business.

PR is made up so so many different components, but finding the right agent is half your battle. Once you have someone playing Robin to your Batman, Gotham is yours!

12

Retail Sales Secrets

Many of us business owners have searched high and low for the secrets to make customers buy more retail and spend more money on services in the salon. I've put together a few of the top hints, tips, and, yes, some of the best-kept secrets in the salon business today.

Think about your last grocery run; what was in the checkout lane with you? Candy and magazines, right? You don't see commodities like bread or baby food in this aisle. What about at the last women's clothing store you went into; nail polish, hand cream, and jewelry? Look closely and you'll see a common thread. These are all small and small-ticket items the retail merchandiser puts there to entice people to spend just a little bit more money on an item that's technically a "luxury," but won't break the bank. I know I've grab up something from the point-of-sale area and tossed it on my pile before, I see other people doing it every time I shop, and I'm sure you do it, too. In your salon, the haircut, updo, color job, or mani-pedi is the big-ticket commodity people are coming in to get, but if you display and talk about your retail products correctly, you can upsell almost every purchase, sending people home with products they may not have thought they needed, but that they're going to enjoy!

On the counter at the typical salon, there is a variety of cheap items, which I call the pocket stuffers, that are generally twenty bucks and under. How many of us have grabbed up a pocket stuffer, just thinking, "That's pretty," or "So-and-so would like this." I know I have. These are also the items you're going to reach for if you get cornered by a salesperson who is really sweet and spends a lot of time with you, to the point you feel bad not buying anything.

Since the pocket-stuffer phenomenon is so common and effective in retail, make sure you always have an array of small items in beautiful packaging, priced right, up at the counter where your clients check in and out. Have your receptionist point them out and talk about why they are fun or valuable products.

So, the point of purchase is a great place to boost brisk sales of small items, but what about the more expensive and high-end products? The bottles of shampoo you sell for $29.95 that really nourishes hair; how are you going to get clients to spring for that shampoo—and the conditioner on top of it!—if they're used to paying much less for the off-brand at the drug store? Not easy, but it can be done!

Retailers have come up with many ways to entice us into getting into the buying mode. I call them buying secrets! These little secrets enable them to get the hardest customer to stop, look at, and even touch retail they may never have had any desire to buy.

Even the toughest customer deep down wants to make a purchase they think will make them feel or look good.

I encourage you to put these selling tactics to work in your retail environment.

Invoke Science—The best thing you can do in your business is to establish a dress code for your salespeople who will be selling products. Clinique came up with the best marketing idea ever created: They put their salespeople in white lab coats. People are trained to respect what experts in white lab coats have to say. A cosmetic counter salesperson in a white lab coat capitalizes on that dynamic and establishes his or her expertise. Of course, the salespeople have to actually be well versed in the products they are selling, but it's a surefire way to sell beauty products.

Also, if your product supplier or representative gave you marketing materials, like brochures with charts or illustrations of how a product works on the hair strand microscopically, be sure to point these out to customers. People want to be able to visualize a product working and have a mental image of the result. That mental image they get from charts, diagrams, and illustrations is going to be far more convincing than a salesperson's recommendation alone.

Play the Expert—Play on the philosophy of the brands your selling. Explain in detail the long list of proven facts about your products and have a list of any of today's stars who may be using these brands. If they're using it, your clients will probably see that as a sign the product is effective.

More Expensive Equals Better—A product that's priced two times higher than anything else must be better than any other brand

and symbolizes a certain status. Of course, high-priced items gain a reputation as being the best. The "if it's more expensive, it must be better" mentality trick is one of the oldest in retailing, but still works today.

Many of us have been bitten by the anti-aging bug. If we spend on a hair gel or makeup that cost more, many of us think it will make us feel better and look younger than the lower-priced products. Also, being able to make that purchase is a way of saying we have worked hard and we owe that much to ourselves.

Go For the Nose—This is a clever trick, but many retailers today pump certain smells into the air to put you into the buying frame of mind. Certain department stores rely on coconut fragrance to help sell bathing suits. Infant apparel gets the baby powder smell and lingerie gets a lilac or lavender aromatherapy-like smell.

In a salon retail environment, lighting a few scented candles can give your salon or retail store the exact smell you are trying to get in your store. The more pleasurable you make the shopping experience, the more likely your customers are to stay longer and buy more. How many times have you found yourself buying something that smelled so good you had to have it?

Music to Your Ears—Many retail stores play music to keep shoppers relaxed, giving them a calm, soothing feeling, which keeps them in a happy frame of mind. When customers are happy, they tend to splurge. If you're catering to a older clientele, it makes sense to play Oldies. This will bring them back to happy times in the past. If you cater to a younger generation, it makes sense to play music they listen to, maybe Top 40s plus some Indie songs. To compromise between the two, you can always go with soft, soothing elevator or yoga music.

Make the Puzzle Pieces Fit—Whether you're a big retailer or a small mom and pop, make all the parts come together. If you're offering makeup, let your shoppers see how all the parts come together. Eyeliner, lipstick, and blush should all be in one section. You do not want clients wandering around your store, trying to figure out how to get ready for a night on the town. Make it simple, keep it close, and make sure the price is right. Let the entire makeover fit in their budget. Then, don't let them leave without everything, or at least the key pieces, to recreate their makeover.

It also makes sense to have a mannequin dressed from head to toe, dripping in accessories. The more they see how the end result will look when they are finished the more they will spend. Buyers like to see what they may look like by imagining themselves in what you have on display or on your shelves.

Make It Shine—What draws your eye more, a diamond ring or a plain gold band? No contest! It's almost a physical response. Humans automatically look as an item that shimmers and assume something that gleams is fancy and valuable. If you want to be successful in retail, your counters and every surface that products rest on must gleam and shine. Give the customer the impression your products are worth every penny your selling them for.

Bargain Sale—We all want a bargain. Big retailers have had door-buster days for years. The morning after Thanksgiving has been a retailer's dream for as far back as I can remember. Why is it that customers feel compelled to rush to the store to buy the same thing they could get the day before, which may not be rare or even valuable? It's the high of knowing they're getting a deal. Stores take advantage of this feeling by turning their sales into adrenaline-charged events.

Your business can also offer these one-day sales or door busters. Let your clients know that you are planning an event; tell them you will be dropping prices on special, popular items. Email them, call them, send a postcard, post it, text it, Tweet it, make it an extravaganza! There is no reason your fun little event can't give the customers the same adrenaline rush the big stores do, with the same type of results.

13

Retail Store No-No's

When we decide to open a salon retail section, there are so many aspects of the business we should know before jumping in, plus the things we'll learn as we go along. Call it what you will, but learning as you go can be quite expensive and frustrating. The learn-as-you-go approach can be avoided if you follow some very easy steps I'm going to discuss in this chapter.

We all know a bad retail store experience when we see it. I'm sure at one point in your life, you've walked into a store and immediately felt compelled to turn around and walk out the door. Maybe it was on a long trip with the family and you stopped at a country store. To your dismay, the place was dirty and disheveled, the inventory looked old and dusty, and on top of that, the bathrooms were filthy.

I remember visiting a really expensive women's clothing store, looking for a birthday present for my wife. A friend had raved about this store, but the minute I walked in, I had a feeling this retail experience was going to be a disaster.

At first I didn't know if anyone was even working in the store; it was empty. The lighting was dim and oppressive and the music was blasting. The racks of clothes were so cluttered I was knocking things off just walking around. I poked around for a few minutes, feeling uncomfortable, until a really young saleswoman appeared from the back.

I thought I was saved and might get some help finding a gift quickly, but no. This saleswoman was more of a hindrance than a help; she didn't know the prices on any of the unmarked items and wouldn't lift a finger to find them out. She also didn't know if the items I had picked up came in more sizes or not. Would it have been so hard to walk to the back or the computer to check? No, but it was too much for this saleswoman. I told her flat out that I had expected more from this place, based on its reputation, and she said she would mention that to her boss, but her body language was saying, "And I care because?"

What a customer's nightmare! And a retailer's nightmare, too, since *this* customer is never setting foot in that place again. Does any of this ring a bell? These are common retailing no-no's that can easily be avoided.

Retail is about detail. Every day, retailers small and large forget about small details that cost next to nothing. Most retail store owners are obsessed with management issues like pricing, marketing, inventory, and employees. On top of that, owners are trying to juggle personal and professional life. Sound familiar?

However, when a customer visits your store, he or she isn't thinking about any of these challenges that you face, because he or she is thinking about a pleasant buying experience. In other words, you can do all the big things right and still get it wrong, if you don't pay attention to the little things that contribute to an enjoyable buying experience for your customers. Sure, work/life balance is important, but keep in mind that you can't have work/life balance if your business goes under and you're out of work!

Lack of Cleanliness—Cleanliness is the number one item any retail store must have. All customers expect a retail store to be clean. They look for this when they enter your store. Dirty floors, water stained ceilings, and messy or dusty shelves signal that a business is in trouble and may cause customers to quickly retreat and shop somewhere else. No one wants to walk into the neighborhood crazy cat lady's house and step in dust and hairballs! The same is true for your salon.

You also have to consider treatment rooms, bathrooms, and any dressing rooms. These rooms may be mostly hidden from clients, but once they see or step inside these places, paying customers can immediately transform into retreating customers. If anything, these areas should be more spotless compared to the rest of your retail store. Cleaning only takes a little time each day your salon is open. There's so little cost involved and shame on you if this is not a priority!

Poor Ambiance—The ambiance of your retail store should match the retail you are selling. If you are a very high-end salon and the retail you are selling is expensive and considered the best in the industry, the ambiance in your store should be that of an overall wonderful, clean, relaxing environment. I envision soft, warm colors and soothing music that make the experience something your clients will enjoy and remember, plus will put them in a buying mood. If your staff is playing music better suited for a sleazy bar, this will be offensive to your customers. When your clients walk in your place of business, does it smell like chemicals or today's lunch? If so, your clients will find that off-putting as well. Since these are important issues for the people who shop in your store, they need to become important issues to you as well.

Low Lighting—Retailing is all about being able to display the products you are selling in the most beautiful setting, as well as giving your customers the ability to experience what they're buying with their senses. Customer can't buy what they can't see. Bright overhead lighting is standard in most retail spaces. Replace burnt-out bulbs and clean the windows before you even notice dirt, so natural light can illuminate the retail area and allow your clients to see the merchandise. Poor lighting casts a depressing pall over your store's interior, which clients will want to escape. I'll talk about this more in Chapters 21 and 22.

Handwritten Signs—In this era of technology, there is no reason to display handwritten signage to promote a sale or markdown on a special item. You do *not* have to have a PhD in marketing to use your computer and printer to generate signage for your retail sales or specials. Handwritten signs simply look tacky and give the feeling that your business is simply running on life support.

Filthy Restrooms—Expect your restrooms to be a high-traffic area, especially if you want clients to stay long enough to peruse your retail section. Bathrooms deserve to be in the top of the list when it comes to a good retail environment. Nobody wants to use a restroom that smells and looks like it hasn't been cleaned for a year.

Bathrooms should also never be used as storage space for your merchandise. Why would anyone want to buy something that is stored in a public bathroom? Put it in the back room! Stock up on essentials like toilet paper, soap, and trash bags, and clean the restrooms daily or twice daily.

Crowded Aisles—Consumers like a large selection when shopping, but also don't want to feel like they can't move around the aisles freely. Aisles that are packed with unopened boxes, or with merchandise stacked too high, have an impact on what and how much clients purchase. If they can't get to the products easily, they'll simply decide your retail environment is to difficult to shop in. It's hard enough to get clients into your retail area; the last thing you want to do is drive them away, because they feel cramped or uncomfortable.

Inaccurate Pricing—One of the worst things you can do when selling retail is not have the correct prices on items you are displaying for sale. If you are selling beauty retail products, you may have several of the same items for sale on your shelves. It is never a good business practice to have different prices on the same products, so be careful to re-mark every single item, if you need to re-price a particular product. If you miss one, the customer should always get the lower price; that's your problem, if you don't check each item before putting them out for sale.

Check Out, Not Get-Me-Out—The check-out area is the focal point of your business. It's usually the first place the customer makes contact with your business and the last. If you want to make a good impression on your clients, you don't want to give them a feeling your check out area is too cluttered, busy, or hard to navigate.

Part Two

When You Need
to
Make a Change

14

How to Attract New Clients Every Day

There's no secret to being successful in the bread and butter of the salon industry. Creating and developing a larger and expanded client base will likely mean you'll be making more money at the end of the day. The challenge we have as cosmetologists and salon owners is finding new customers. If we each had a genie in a lamp and we could use just one wish a year to get a hundred new clients, we wouldn't have to bother with painstakingly trying to grow our client base each and every day.

Developing and growing your client base is not easy. It takes constantly creating new ideas and marketing strategies, which your competitor is also trying to do, for greater market share. The person who comes up victorious is the usually one who works the hardest and is constantly on the move. I like to use the expression: The early bird catches the worm. We have all heard it. What it comes down to is the person who is eager enough to try new things, work a little harder, maybe work a little later, and constantly put out a hand to meet new people, wins.

Let's take a look at various ways to attract new customers.

1. Advertising is key, and the way to advertise successfully is to generate promising leads in exchange for the money you spend. To do so, it helps to offer a message that not only hits on your target customers, but also showcases the value you can offer them.

   Take television, for example. In general, TV will be your most expensive option. But targeting based on programming instead of channels or networks—that is, placing ads on "Cooking with Joe" versus a campaign on a cooking network—offers a more specific outlet for your resources.

2. Radio also allows you to selectively target formats and programming. Even in large metro areas, you can often score inexpensive sponsorships of weather or traffic reports.

3. Newspaper subscribership has dwindled in recent years but, depending on your market; they're still a worthy option for attracting new customers. If your target market is, say, people aged 55 or older, you may want to consider community or city papers, or niche publications, as older consumers still rely on them for information.

4. Postcard mailings is another alternative to reach out to an exclusive target market. This is a good way to target a specific region within proximity of your salon's business. There are local companies that mail out multiple businesses' advertisements in their packets. This is a very inexpensive way to target a market and also get introduced to other businesses and see how they are advertising as well.

But even older people are increasingly turning to the Web—making it a definite jumping-off point for any advertising strategy. To tap into this medium, your first step is to establish a Web presence, if you don't have one already. Then, depending on your target customer—consumers at large or other businesses—pick your Web channel. LinkedIn, for instance, is a mainstay for businesses, CEOs, and other owners and entrepreneurs, while Facebook is wildly popular among consumers, and Twitter and Instagram among young people.

5. Networking and referrals are the most cost-effective way to expand your business. All it takes is your time and good social skills, going to networking and charity events. Parties of friends and family are also excellent ways of creating a bigger client base. Landing referrals from networking or past business associations isn't just a cheap way to pick up new business, it's also a way to pick up clients with the highest retention rates. What's more, referral customers tend to purchase more over time and in turn become a source of additional referrals.

How do you find referrals? Beyond having a product or service that's in demand, you must have a clear idea of who your "perfect" or "ideal" client is. That way, you can communicate to others in your network that you're trying to meet the needs, wants, or desires of that very specific client profile.

Then, you need to ask for referrals from satisfied customers. Be sure to find ways to continually thank your sources for their ongoing advocacy of your business.

6. Another way to leverage available resources is through what's known as a "host-beneficiary" arrangement; basically, teaming up. In this scenario, another business with the same target customer will use their database to promote your business. They might attach a gift voucher or other discount offer for

your products at the end of one of a newsletter or mailing. Examples of this include:

- The local coffee shop puts postcards or business cards promoting your business on the counter.
- A restaurant in town promotes your salon as well as you giving each other referral business.
- The local gym promotes your salon by advertising their gym in your salon as well. This works out very well for personal trainers promoting each other's services.

To draw in another business, offer to pay for the business owner's mailing or email expenses, or offer the business owner commission on any sales. Sharing expenses is a common way to target each other's customer bases without a big marketing expenses.

7. You might take that partnership a step further and form what's known in the industry as a "strategic alliance." While a host beneficiary relationship is generally a one-time or short-term commitment, strategic alliances can sometimes last for many years. For instance, a Web designer and an ad agency might send each other referrals and work hand in hand together. As long as there's continued value to the shared audience, strategic alliances produce streams of referral business, which is ultimately what will benefit you most.

15

Looking for Clients? Don't Give Up So Soon!

When you're just starting out as a salon owner or independent stylist, or even if you're an old pro, it can be frustrating looking for new clients. You've read this book. You've started implementing some of the *Ready, Set, Go!* ideas. You've made calls. You've sent letters. You've schmoozed at business meetings and social events. Yet, nothing seems to happen fast enough. The clients just don't seem to be knocking down the salon doors.

My advice? Don't give up too soon. Anything good takes time. How much is really up to you!

I recently got a call from a salon owner who was struggling to attract clients. He was on the verge of giving up.

"What have you done so far?" I asked.

"Well," he said, "I got my Web site up, I sent out 100 postcards to promote it, and I went to a Chamber of Commerce meeting.

"That's great!" I said. "What else?"

There was a pause. Then he said sheepishly, "Well, that's all I've done so far."

There are 365 days in a year. Even if you have read the *Ready, Set, Go!* books, it would be impossible to implement all these ideas in a short period of time. Fact! These ideas do work but, yes, they take time to work. It would be impossible to implement every one of them in a single phase. When you do start, expect things to happen gradually. It's way too early to give up, because you have plenty of time to plan and take action. Even if you still don't know what you want to get out of the year, you still have time to figure it out and get started. All good things don't happen in a New York minute. Sorry, this is a process.

Often, when you're marketing your business or services, things don't happen measurably at first. Even if you send out 1,000 postcards, visit every Starbucks in town with card in hand, or cold call until your voice grows hoarse, it can take lots of time and lots of marketing activity before you begin to see results.

There are many reasons for this:

- A client may be interested in visiting with you, but hasn't had a chance or opportunity to call you yet. It can take months before the opportunity arises to give you a call and book an appointment. For example, a few months ago, I was hired by a consulting firm whose head picked up and read my first book five years ago (he kept it that long!).
- You need to build up a level of familiarity and trust before new clients will visit you. They need to hear from you, read your blog, see your Web site, walk by your salon, see your marketing material, review your samples, see you at events, and get

to know you. All that takes time. If you give up after just two contacts, you'll never get new clients.

- A client may be impressed with your services, but they're using another stylist, barber, and or manicurist. Don't walk away. Your turn might come. I often ask clients like these if I can be number two. Many appreciate having a backup style expert.

- It takes more marketing activity than a lot of salon owners think to attract clients. One very successful salon owner once told me that she makes an average of one hundred cold calls, to a well-researched list of prospects, before she nails a new client. This may seems excessive, but it works for her and the salon she owns is extremely successful. Not only that, her staff is booked solid and they are happy as larks.

- It can take a while to create what I call "marketing momentum." If you start doing a lot of things to promote your services, after a while that has a snowball effect and you start to really get results. But if you give up too early, the snowball crumbles, or in this case, melts!

It takes a lot of time and hard work to attract new clients. Don't let anyone tell you differently. There are no shortcuts, no magic bullets, no genies waiting in lamps. You just have to keep at it and keep improving what you're doing. Never stop. Remember there are 365 days in the year. Start today; you've got 364 days left!

When I hung out my shingle as a freelance writer and salon business consultant many years ago, I got my first client fairly quickly. I was lucky. However, it took six frustrating months before I got my second client! Yes, it was discouraging, more often than I care to admit, but if I had given up too soon, you wouldn't be reading this book.

16

Girlfriends' Night Out Brings in New Business

In today's world, many of us business owners struggle to think of new ways to attract business. The new customer treadmill is something we have to continually think about in the salon business to be successful. You can spend tons of your hard-earned money on marketing and sometimes end up with poor results. There are other avenues to gain customers, so sometimes just thinking out of the box a bit can be easier and more successful than the old-school marketing techniques.

Many salons are trying to convey to their customers they're trend-setters. Not only with being specialists in hair and makeup, but also with clothing, jewelry, and accessories. Fashionistas today see new trends through various channels, on television, magazines, and on social media. They want what they see, when they see it, and they see more of it and faster than ever.

The going theory about shopping today is that people in general want their clothes, jewelry, and home décor fast, but also with convenience in mind. In most households, two or more people are working, so it's not easy for someone to just take a day to go shopping.

Amazon.com and other online companies are now offering same-day delivery in some communities, just to keep up with the demands of the customers, so the customers never have to leave the couch. What does that mean for salons, though?

Girls' Night Out

Salons around the country are trying to fill the void of not only regular customers but new ones as well. By offering girls'-night-out "trunk shows" or "jewelry sales," salons are creating fun, special events for women to enjoy as quality time together. First, you select a special date and time, usually on a slow night, so as not disrupt regular business or compete with the draw of restaurants, movie theaters, or bars on Friday and Saturday nights. Then, you send invites to existing clients, with an emphasis on them bringing a friend or two.

Forgive me for making a blanket statement, but it seems pretty clear to me that women are wired for relationships. That means these girls'-night-outs should be geared toward relationship building. Make sure plenty of staff members are on hand, so no one is left alone. The clothing lines you bring in or jewelry should be in various sizes and styles that cater to everyone. Trying on blouses, dresses, jeans, shoes, and jewelry is pleasurable and entertaining, when the atmosphere is just right, so have some wine and cheese sitting out, let your customers ply each other with drinks, shop, and have a blast! The night out will be a memorable one.

Social Selling

This form of selling retail, outside of traditional retail stores, is a growing trend. The success of social selling is because most woman these days don't have time to shop with other people. Often they have children tagging along behind them while shopping.

Trying to shop cuts into family and personal time, and girl-friend time is usually the first thing that gets cut out of a working mom or working woman's busy schedule. Yet most yearn for input when shopping, especially for trendy new clothes, jewelry, and makeup. Many times people lack the confidence to buy something new and different. If these overworked moms can leave the kids at home with a babysitter some weeknight, or the non-moms can leave work on time one evening, to spend some quality time with their friends, you have set up a win-win situation. They're happy to be shopping at a relaxing, fun event, and you're happy they're shopping, too!

Another nice thing about these girls'-night-outs is that you and your staff can interact with people, offering advice. "Does this look good?" "How should I do my hair if I wear this?" "How about eyeliner to match this eyeshadow?" These are all cool ways to connect with new people and introduce your salon's services and staff to your guests.

The absolute best part about girls'-night-outs for you is that many of clothes may have to be ordered, so guess what! Your clients and their guests will have to come back to the salon to pick up their purchases. Mission accomplished. When they come back, it's time to sell your new acquaintances on the salon and your services. What a great opportunity to open the door to potential new business. Good luck and have some fun!

17

How You Can Compete with the Big Chains

It took you many years of working hard behind the chair to build your client base. You saved as much money as you could by keeping focused with one thing in mind, managing your own salon. The planning went on for two years, meeting with real-estate companies trying to find the best location, with the demographics that best suited you and your clients, salon designers, furniture companies, Web designers, and finally the last piece of the puzzle; meeting your local bank to nail down the necessary financing to make it all happen.

Finally the day had come; after a successful grand opening party, you were open for business. All of your planning paid off! You were now exactly in the position you wanted to be; on the road to becoming a successful salon owner.

The fanfare in your town was overwhelming. Your existing clients were so excited and a steady flow of new customers seemed to be coming in daily. Wow, just what you dreamed of!

Then, in the blink of an eye, a big chain opened right around the corner from your salon, charging half what you charge. You never expected this to happen. What do you do? Hand over the keys to your salon, throw up the white flag, and surrender? You have never been a quitter, so that option is out, but how do you compete with someone who is bigger, stronger, and has deeper pockets than you? Let's take a look at how you and your salon can compete with the big chains in today's business world.

Small business owners naturally feel anxious when a large chain store threatens their business. The idea of having to compete with large retailers keeps many would-be entrepreneurs from ever opening a salon in the first place. Unfortunately, those fears are well-founded. Studies show people now purchase a higher percentage of their merchandise from mass merchandisers and consequently a lower percentage from local merchants. Also, the demographics of the area your salon is located will dictate the percentage of people who prefer service price over quality.

It may be daunting, but despite the emergence of these multi-million dollar businesses, many small retailers continue to thrive (and profit) in a highly competitive marketplace. Remember, those huge businesses were small once, too, and they just did a lot of things right. You can, too. The key to survival is to offer products and services your competition does not. Implement strategies to overcome the lower prices and wider selection that large retailers provide. Here are some tips to better position your salon and retail business for competing with the big box stores.

Don't Panic—Occasionally, we can be our own worst enemy. Talk of a big competitor coming to your community is not a reason to immediately consider relocating or closing your business. First, recognize that you may need to make a positive change in the way you do business. Then, assess whether or not you have the desire to make those changes. If you have invested the time, energy and money to open your business then changes are a normal part of doing what is necessary for survival. If you are not open to change, then your salon will die a slow death. Not to mention taking you and your personal finances with it.

Do the Research—Seek advice from your trade association or consider hiring an industry consultant to conduct a formal study of what customers value most and what they value least about your business. Speak to your product manufacturer's sales reps. They should be able to assist you with a true understanding of what you need to sell in your salon, when it comes to retailing.

You also need to come up with a plan to counter-attack the big box store with items they don't sell. Understand your store's competitive edge. Don't be afraid to shop your competition. One way to be educated about the way your competition does business is by experiencing their customer service first hand. If possible, talk to their customers. Find out what their shoppers like or dislike about the chain store. Visit the store several times with and without your staff to see exactly what you need to do and offer, to be a better service and retail provider to your customer base.

Dare to Be Different—Mass merchandisers generally have a little of everything, whereas smaller specialty stores can focus on a narrow but lucrative niche. This can establish your store as the place to go when buying these items. If your market niche is very small, consider keeping a few products and services that appeal to a wider range of customers, but keep exceptional product depth.

Education is key, so your staff needs to understand the retail products your salon uses and sells. If the big box store sells the same products as your salon, you may think about dropping your current brands and finding another. By doing this you are now different than the big box store. Find a manufacturer who is willing to help you grow your business with a new product offering. If you choose to stick with the retail brands you currently use, then you better become the specialist in these brands and know the ins and outs of the products. Knowledge is key to overcoming your competitors when trying to beat them at the retailing game.

Focus on what makes your business unique. Emphasize the originality of your inventory as compared to the offerings of the chain store. Customers are intrigued by the unusual and are often attracted to the idea of getting something special from an independently owned business. Smaller retail businesses also have the luxury of creating a comfortable, cozy atmosphere within their store, which is often lacking at the big stores.

Let your customers touch, feel, smell, and use the product before the purchase. Explain in detail how they will look when they use these products at home. Give them a money-back guarantee, in case they aren't happy with the products. These little things will go a long way with your customer base.

Most big box stores do not let customers open any of their retailing products, never mind letting you try the products before you buy. These little tactics that are so simple will separate your salon form the larger chains. Customer service has to always be a top priority with you and your staff.

Hours of Operation—It's hard enough to juggle running a salon, staff, clients, accounting, and your family and social life. I feel your pain; owning and operating a business is no easy task. The idea of keeping more hours may have you wondering if salon ownership is worth it.

Currently, most families are two-income households. Your customers may also be working crazy hours, as well as further away from home, to make ends meet. Regular 9-to-5 operating hours and being closed on Sunday and Monday are no longer feasible, if you want to be successful in the salon business.

I'm not saying you have to be open 24 hours a day, 365 days a year, but to have a successful, profitable salon, you must be ready to meet the needs of your clients.

Let's look at an example: If your salon is located in a city, next to a train or bus station, it would make sense to open earlier and stay open later to be able to serve the clients who may be stopping by on the way to or from work for a quick blowout or bottle of their favorite anti-frizz serum.

If your salon is located next to a police station, factory, hospital, or other business that has employees working in shifts, keeping your salon open later may be a way for clients to get the much-needed service they can't fit into their busy schedules.

There is a reason big box retailers are open late at night or early in the morning. Speak to your customers; ask if opening early or closing later would help them with their schedules. If you don't ask, you will never know. The worst thing in the salon ownership world is when your client pulls up to your salon and the lights are out and the sign on the door says, "Closed." No doubt, they'll be on their way to the store that's open, to get their favorite hair care products or at least settle for something close to what they buy from you. If this happens often, don't be surprised if they don't come back. Convenience and ease win every time.

The Power of Pricing—Be open to a little haggling where price is concerned. More price negotiating goes on in your typical mom-and-pop shops than in the big box stores. Bargain shoppers know the independent retailer has the power to negotiate a sale, so these customers are more inclined to shop where they feel they set their own prices. Remember, it is all about the customer's perception.

One of the keys to successful retailing in your salon comes down to your relationships with your suppliers. Using them as true partners will enable you to run specials and offer incentives to new and existing clients. Most salons do not leverage their relationships with their product salespeople. Not taking advantage and understanding what the role of a true product sales representative is a huge mistake.

Product retail sales reps call on your salon not only to take necessary orders but to educate your staff, let you know when the manufacturer is coming out with new products, and tell you when they're running a promotion on other products.

These business partners can give you retailing signage, promotional pieces for your display cases, retail bags for purchases, and transparencies for your windows, promoting the brands you sell. If you don't bother to ask and truly leverage this relationship, then your success in retail will be minimal at best. This is a true cause of failure in many salons. I'm going to talk more about this relationship in the next chapter.

Personal Attention—Treat each client as your favorite client. As a small business owner, you can concentrate on the little details. Superb customer service is the biggest intangible asset to the independent business. People like to shop and have their services done where they feel comfortable and where they feel the owner truly cares about their wants and needs. It's the least expensive change to make in order to take on the larger chain stores. Offering a true five-star experience in your salon doesn't cost you anything. It's just a matter of implementing this business philosophy, one client at a time, every time.

Building Relationships—Big-box stores can't offer the personal touch of a mom-and-pop, so why not capitalize on that fact? People prefer doing business in a warm environment with someone they like, feel comfortable with, and have the ability to open up to. Have you ever seen anyone go talk to the clerk in the big-box check-out line, when then need to vent about a relationship in shambles or when their job isn't going well? I thought not. Have you ever seen people come to their stylist when they need to talk it out? Probably daily, am I right?

The simple art of listening transmits a message that you truly care about your clients, just like a warm handshake, a pat on the back, or hand-written thank-you notes with special offers for the next visit. Greeting customers by name, taking customer calls promptly, and making exceptions that large retailers can't make, will help your smaller storefront stand out.

Connect with Locals Using Social Media—Large chains and franchises typically do a terrible job of maintaining social media profiles in the local communities where they have stores. Set yourself apart by ramping up local engagement via Facebook, Twitter, Pinterest, Instagram, and YouTube. Post pictures of your staff and clients, your fun events, and promotions your salon is currently offering.

Blog Locally—If the big boys even have a blog, they're not likely spending time focusing on local issues. By frequently blogging about topics your local customers actually care about, you increase your salon's odds of generating positive local search results online. Plus, you're telling your customers they should have more—not less—information about the products and services you sell.

Support Local Causes—National chains move slowly, especially when it comes to sponsoring or supporting local events. As a local yourself, pay attention to what's coming up on the local events calendar and join up with civic-minded organizations that are targeting the same people who might like to buy your products or services. Supporting local causes endears your brand among your target demographic. The best part of being small is you can choose who you want to support. Supporting a local dance school or kid's soccer team will go a long way with your clients and hopefully bring in new business.

State Your Differences as Positives—Don't bash the competition in front of your staff or with customers. That makes you look like your back is against the wall and you're lashing out. Instead, point out the clear differences between your offerings by speaking in positives, not negatives. For example, "Featuring locally-sourced ingredients that are healthy for you, your hair, and your family since 1997," is a better message than "Buy local!" or "You call *that* organic?" Similarly, "Client-focused and ready to meet your needs!" comes off better than, "They don't care about you, your hair, or your family!"

You're trying to come across as the superior business, so be the superior person, too. Spread positive energy and messages about your business; then your clients will feel at ease, realizing your business is here to stay because it's a great place full of great people.

Use Size to Your Advantage—In most cases, every product you see on the shelves of a big box or chain store, or being sold or offered by a franchise, is there because it went through a long, long approvals process and one person at the top—a national buyer or category manager—okayed it. You, however, can start selling a new item at a moment's notice. By specializing in the niche items that helped you build your enterprise, you'll continue to drive business in your direction. Change is good; don't be afraid to switch things up to meet the demands of your customers.

Salon Employees' Success Strategies—In order to keep your employees from defecting to the competition or staging a salon staff walkout, you must treat your staff fairly and better than the big-box can treat them. Motivate your staff and pay attention to their needs. Help your staff become proficient in their respective departments and make sure they are readily available to meet your customers' needs. If your employees can provide top-tier service, your customers will have an extra incentive to continue doing business with you, which will circle back around and keep your employees working hard and keep morale high.

Bring Some Hustle

These tips for competing with big box stores can help level the playing field. However, don't be misled into thinking exceptional customer service or unique products will win out over lower prices every time. As our customers' shopping and service-selection habits change, so should our thinking. To succeed, you and I and all small business owners must lead or keep pace with the change. With or without new retail competition, this kind of planning is something small businesses have to be doing consistently.

18

How Your Distributor Can Grow Your Business

Building a better, more profitable business doesn't come from only focusing on your salon space, equipment, marketing, and staff. Yes they are all very important working parts of your salon's success, but I can't tell you the number of salons today that forget about one very important ingredient, the ingredient that can mean the difference between struggling and not making money, and quickly turning a profit. Retail!

If you're selling it I commend you, but are you selling it at a profit? Or are you currently overbuying, selling at a loss, over-pricing it, or are you under-utilizing your distributor?

Your distributor relationship can really help build your business. If you're not making a profit on retail, I'll show you how you can quickly turn your retail side-work into a profit center in your salon. I'll go into more retail detail in the next chapter, and you've heard me talk about it a dozen times before (ahem, only because it's crucial!), but first you have to understand your distributor is here to help with your salon's success. Without their help, it's going to be difficult to turn a profit by selling retail.

The first thing you need to do is look at what products you're selling. Are you selling multiple lines of products? Which products are you selling the most? Do any products just sit on your shelves? Do you have a back room full of inventory that isn't moving? Does your staff use the products you sell and are they educated enough to sell these products? Does your salon software keep track of inventory and what products your clients buy?

All this seemed easy when you opened your salon, right? Who knew running your business could be so complicated? It may seem hard, but it gets easier when you properly take advantage of a relationship you may not be utilizing.

Anatomy of a Distributor—The first thing you have to understand is that your distributor has a good sales team and what the team wants is products they can sell easily. These salespeople may sell multiple lines of products. The goal is to outfit your salon with these products. Simply put, the more they sell, the more they make. Everyone's happy, right? Wrong! If it were that easy, you wouldn't be reading this book.

Salespeople working for the distributor work on a combination of salary and commission. Their success is based on your salon's success. Normally, these sales people migrate to the salons that really understand selling retail and they'll go out of their way to help these salons' owners build their retail business and run a profitable salon.

Generally speaking, these representatives work on the 80/20 rule, where 80% of their business comes from 20% of the salons they do business with. The other salons just buy what they need, don't ask for help, and most likely don't push retail sales. These salons usually fly by the seat of their pants and don't make a profit. These salons are not on the weekly call list with their salesperson and usually get lost in the shuffle. Sound familiar?

Okay, so now you understand how the distributor and their sales team work and what they're looking for from you, the salon owner. Now it's time to foster a rapport that will help you dig out of your rut and help you reach your salon's goals, creating a stronger, more profitable business.

Take the Bull by the Horns—Time is running out. Don't delay making an appointment with your distributor or the salesperson who handles your salon. Most of these salespeople report to a district manager. Ask to see both in your meeting. Remember, your business is on life support, so an extra person who understands the salon business will be more than helpful in this meeting.

The meeting should take place in the salon before you open. Your staff doesn't need to know your affairs, so they don't need to be there.

When you do meet, you have to be completely honest with your salesperson and distributor; explain what's going on with your business and that you're struggling to stay afloat. Please remember, the next step is closing the salon, so any suggestion is worth listening to. Put aside your ego so you can be open minded and ready for change.

New Ideas—There are many things that will come from your meeting. The topics you should be discussing should be tactics that will bring dramatic and quick results. Remember, you need to make money quickly to increase your bottom line.

Although your distributor team doesn't have a crystal ball and will not be able to turn your salon around after the first meeting, they should be able to come up with some quick ideas to get your salon moving in the right direction. Find out the full array of services your distributor has to offer that could give you dramatic results. Ideas to discuss and put into action are:

- Giving away samples
- Carrying the number-one-selling products
- Putting in newer product displays
- Getting marketing material for your shelves, window displays, front desk signage, retailing shopping bags with the product logos on them
- On-time inventory and management, i.e. the ability to buy as you need it. Do not overbuy until you get your salon on its feet. You don't need to spend thousands on new products.
- Immediate staff education and training on all products sold in the salon
- Incentives on product volume based on what your salon sells
- Front desk education on retailing
- Inventory and potential sales growth based on current and future sales
- Upcoming deals on new products
- Online advertising of your salon
- Financing terms
- Business partner services that your distributor may be affiliated with, such as credit card processors, salon equipment dealers, software companies, and finance companies
- Returns or buyouts of old products for new
- Planning a salon event focused on the brands your distributor is selling

These are all great ideas to help rocket-up sales. The key is to make sure you react and get them put into place.

Be an Active Participant—Distributors and their sales team are more likely to provide great service if you uphold your end as a timely payer and avid communicator. Have a clear understanding of their policies and procedures, so when you need a favor or improvements more help, they continue to be there for you. In time, as your salon starts to turn the corner, you should be able to take advantage of better pricing on products, terms, and any new promotions you may not have been offered, due to performance and volume.

In Short—How can you get your distributor on board when you need them the most?

- Commit to one brand or manufacturer
- Put their products front and center in your salon
- Educate your salon staff to promote the brands you're selling
- Get to know your salespeople and make them part of your team
- Communicate openly
- Be honest
- Ask for their ideas and business smarts, before it's too late

19

How to Get Your Retail Sales Off Life Support

On your way to work, you pass several salons in your area, some bigger than the one you own, others smaller. You notice that one has a garbage dumpster out front and is under major renovation. Another is open earlier than yours and already has clients coming in. The salon closest to you is next door to a Starbucks and is said to be the busiest salon in town. You always dreamed of being the go-to salon, but something seems to be missing. You work your tail off, but no matter what you do, you can't seem to get your salon business moving. Sometimes it seems your salon is stuck in the idle position, or is going in reverse.

When results count, you'll find that highly successful people aren't any more talented or intelligent than you are; they simply have learned how to do things in a different and more profitable way. The salon next door or around the corner may not be as beautiful as yours or doesn't have the talented stylists your salon does, but they simply understand the art of retailing. The salon experience is fortified through their marketing and understanding their customer's needs. Their retail is priced right and they use their distributor as part of their overall business plan. Simply put, they run their business with a focus on retail and understand the rewards that successful retail brings to the bottom line.

Retail sales is the quickest way to ignite your salon's growth. It could quickly take your salon from breaking even, or worse, to becoming a profitable business in a matter of months.

Let's look at retail from a different angle:

- Retail does not call in sick
- Retail does not have drama
- Retail does not talk back
- Retail does not come in late
- Retail does not have kids to drop off at school
- Retail does not have to go out for a smoke
- Retail does not text or talk on its cellphone
- Retail does not get migraines
- Retail doesn't ask for a higher commission structure weekly
- Retail doesn't require health benefits
- Retail doesn't ask for a 401k, but can certainly add to yours

I don't want to lose focus, so if you're not selling retail, after reviewing the list above, you understand why you should be. If you are, then we'll begin to look at the list I've put together to help you with ideas about getting your customers to buy more retail, which means you'll have a shot at getting your retail department and whole business off life support.

It's not rocket science. You own a salon; you cut and color hair. You should be selling hair-care products as well. If you are already, then you need to sell more. Let's look at ways to have as many customers as possible buy their hair care products at your salon instead of getting the drug store or grocery store brand, or the gigantic bottle of something or another from their membership warehouse.

There is a reason your customers come to your salon. You must be doing something right. It shouldn't be that difficult to convert them into steady retail-buying customers. Here is a winning list of ideas, tips, and techniques to set your business apart and make it a successful one:

A Little Loyalty—Design a loyalty or perk program to turn one-off customers into repeat retail clients. If you plan the program intelligently, then all it takes is printing up a batch of attractively-designed punch cards and investing a very small amount in a special rubber stamp or hole puncher. These days, you could even skip the paper cards and keep track of the loyalty program digitally.

Whether you offer a free bottle of shampoo after a client buys ten, or a free hair- or nail-care product after a certain number of services, it's a great idea to give the customer a freebie punch, stamp, or credit just for starting the program. Make it as easy to use as the coffee shop clubs that capitalize on people's daily coffee habit. Customers use those cards only when the goal seems achievable. I've filled up plenty of those cards myself, but there are loyalty programs I've ditched after the first or second purchase, because the goal seemed too far off.

Branch Out—If you only sell shampoo and conditioner, it's time to branch out into new inventory sectors. Think comprehensive hair care. Try selling a fuller range of the products your distributor offers, such as glosses, gels, anti-frizz serums, and hair sprays with varying levels of stiffness and hold. Display will be key, so choose retail lines that not only offer great products you would use on your own hair, but ones that also have similar-looking packaging, so the client will know all the deep red Redken bottles are in the same line and can be used for the same hair texture.

If you haven't sold cosmetics before, maybe it's time now. The first step is to talk to your staff about the possibility of training them to do make-overs as well as hair, nails, etc. When you know how much enthusiasm there is for new skills for the staff and new services for the clients, talk to different distributors to see who is offering which cosmetic lines, what training they are willing to provide, and what other kinds of support these distributors can offer to you, as you explore new retail territory.

Merchandise Wisely—Instead of arranging the shelves with all the shampoos together and the conditioners in a separate place, display the full range together. This creates visual impact and draws the eye toward the blocks of color in the retail corner. If you have miscellaneous odds and ends, like a vase full of brushes or decorative hair clips, display these items at the counter or have one miscellaneous item at the end of each shelf, sitting next to a product that comes in a range.

What you want to avoid is having one "junk shelf" or baskets of picked-over stuff sitting around. That creates a cluttered look and makes the products seem less special individually. Arrange the shelves to show each item is unique and desirable.

One-Day Sales Events—We all want to feel like we got the best deal out there. Big retailers have had one-day sales events for decades.

Practically every national or cultural holiday in the calendar now comes with the expectation of big sales. Like it or hate it, the phenomenon is here to stay, so capitalize on it yourself! The high of getting something perceived as valuable for a price that's perceived as low makes people feel they've accomplished something, like they've earned the title of Ruler of the Bargain.

Make a plan about how to organize an event, what products to discount, and how to get the word out. Let your clients know you're planning a not-to-be-missed sale; tell them you'll be dropping prices on their favorite items. Email them, call, send a postcard, post it on the door, text it, Tweet it, Facebook it, bring in your buddy who's a DJ, offer hors d'oeuvres and wine tastings—heck, rent a chocolate fountain, if that's what it takes—make it an event they'll tell their friends about!

I talked about retail methods in more detail in "Retail Sales Secrets" in Part One, but here's a quick refresher:

- Set up a professional-looking dress code for your sales team.
- Light a scented candle or spray your work environment with beautifully-scented musk or perfume.
- Play music that suits your audience at all times.
- Keep your counters, shelves, and products shining and clean.
- Remember to make the puzzle pieces fit and group coordinated products together.
- Organize a big discount day or bargain event to boost sales.

20

The All-Important Entrance

We all know how important first impressions are. Our opinion of something or someone is formed quickly upon our first encounter, in as little as seven seconds sometimes! That's why you ought to pay attention to the design of your front door, entrance, and the entire arrival and entry experience when setting up or redesigning your salon. You won't get a second chance, so be sure you present an image that's consistent with the overall layout, design, and aesthetic of your salon.

As the first internal aspect of the salon that you and others' experience, the entrance area needs to reflect, as far as possible, the overall feel you're trying to create for your salon. Findings suggest that your attitude and mood are affected either positively or negatively when entering a place of business, depending on how well the entrance, doors leading into the space, hallway, if any, and reception furniture have been designed and laid out. If these crucial areas are dark, dingy, or cluttered, it creates a negative impact and makes the space feel much smaller and oppressive.

However, in most cases, since the hallway and entrance are areas traffic passes through quickly, they're often treated as an afterthought in the design process. These neglected spaces get stuffed full of simple décor and furnishing (or not) and often become a dumping ground for push-chairs, uncomfortable or overused couches, and shelving from Home Depot or Ikea.

Sure, utilizying this area for storage might make sense to *you*, while solving your retail stock needs, and you may intend to replace them and liven up the area when your salon begins to make money, but there's an issue here. If you're cluttering up your doorway, entrance, and waiting area *today*, your clients are going to get fed up with it *today*, and they might not be back tomorrow.

Many prospective salon clients disappear after Visit One because their first impression didn't live up to what they expected the minute they walked through your salon's doors. In most cases, the styling area or color area aren't visible from the entrance. Yes, your salon may be beautiful beyond that point, but if you need to get the customer there before they can see the beauty of your interior design choices, there's something wrong.

Often, there's only so much you can do with your salon's entrance, but you *can* mitigate problems and design flaws in very inexpensive ways. The salon's hallway needs to be well-lit and welcoming, to make your guests instantly feel relaxed and at home.

Soap and Water Go a Long Way—Cleaning your entrance and wiping down your doorway into the salon is a quick value-add that most people seem to forget.

Painting—A fresh coat of paint goes along way. Pick a distinctive color or finish, or maybe a slick wallpaper. Consider a new color every few years. If your color scheme is more than five years old, go buy a can of paint and get busy!

Add Life—If you have the space in your entrance, add a console or nice piece of furniture and place a live, flowering plant, such as an orchid, or fresh cut flowers. Replace the plant or flowers as needed and keep it fresh.

Accent Pieces—Hang a single, impressive piece of art in the entry. Or, take black-and-white photos of your staff or clients with their best hairstyles; hang them in frames that draw the eye. Make your clients and staff your salon's showpieces.

Light Fixtures—What better place than your entrance to have a grand light fixture to set the mood of your salon? This fixture will become the jewelry of your salon's entrance!

It's essential to always keep not only your clients but also your staff happy. I'm sure your employees would appreciate the lift in spirits they'll get from walking through a fresh, attractive entrance every day. Now that you see the importance of the grand entrance, you can start planning an upgrade in the whole experience.

Inside your salon, it's up to you to create a space that leaves your clients wanting more. The time and investment you make will be worth it. The entrance is not only the first impression your clients have of your salon, it's also the last impression that clients—and staff—take away every time they leave. Remember one thing: Small or large, your entrance space has to hold them in a warm embrace (not a straightjacket)!

21

A Bright Idea: Lighting for the Whole Salon

Light is essential for life, growth, health, beauty, and selling! So much can be done with the direction, color, and intensity of the lighting for your salon. Do you know or have you thought about how lighting affects your clients? To revamp the atomsphere of your salon and cut down on costs, shift your focus to lighting, which can be altered pretty dramatically even without construction or remodeling.

Lighting Creates the Atmosphere of a Room

- Harsh overhead lights create an intimidating feeling and dark shadows.
- Soft, diffused light from around the room, makes it feel safe, warm, and welcoming.

- If your lighting makes your customers uncomfortable—either too bright and harsh or too dark—they will not stick around and spend money.
- Lighting makes your clients' hair shine and gives their skin a smooth and fresh look.
- Lighting not only makes your client look good, but through new lighting systems, like Peter Millard Color Lighting, it will also give your stylist the ability to create the exact color your client is looking for.
- Accent lighting can put your customer in a buying mood by showing off new retail items
- Good lighting will make your clients look gorgeous, and they'll come back for more!

Builders usually only concern themselves with adequate overhead lighting and they may not be thinking how to properly light a salon. In fact, inadequate or improper lighting in a salon environment can have serious consequences and cause the following:

- A dirty or even unsanitary salon
- Safety hazards
- Dissatisfaction with the service results provided by the stylist/colorist/makeup artist
- Clients overlooking products they might otherwise purchase
- Wrong product purchases and the hassle of product exchanges
- Undercharging or overcharging customers
- Mislabeling products or incorrectly placing items on displays
- Poor control over inventory
- An unsafe situation for low-vision customers
- Headaches and eyestrain for your employees

The trick with choosing your lighting is to know enough to make the right decisions for directing your contractors, designers, and/or technicians. You must be involved in these decisions, because your salon's lighting will improve employee productivity, retail sales, safety and security, brand identification, revenue, and profit.

Lighting at Each of the Five Points

Understanding how to use light can make your business much more effective and help you avoid the serious consequences of inadequate lighting. Maintaining and growing a retail business means always showing off the best aspects of your products and services. Therefore, effective lighting is important in all five areas of the business. Here's a look at the Five-Point Salon Lighting Design System areas and some key points about lighting these areas:

Point 1. The Entrance (Doorway/Front Desk/Waiting Area)

- Invites patrons into your salon
- Sets a tone
- Directional lighting helps clients to see when checking out and making appointments

Point 2. Your Product Store (Retail Area)
More details in the next chapter

- Illuminates and spotlights products to get clients' attention
- Helps clients to read product signage, labels, and prices
- Improves sales

Point 3. Your Bread & Butter (Service Area)

- Helps service providers see what they're doing
- Flatters clients' facial features and skin tones
- Provides the right atmosphere for the given service area; for example, massage rooms and spa areas should have dimming capabilities for a more relaxing experience

Point 4. Let Your Color Shine (Color/Dispensary Area)

- Enables clients to see what color the stylist is applying to their hair
- Fewer mistakes, which means higher client satisfaction levels
- Cuts down on phone calls from home from unhappy customers complaining about bad haircuts or hair color
- More engaged staff

Point 5. Behind the Scenes (Utility Area)

- Much-needed lighting for laundry area
- Chemicals for cleaning visible to staff and maintenance people
- Electrical panel or plumbing fixtures visible to all, if needed
- Product/retail storage light needed for inventory control

Remember, there are times when you'll want to have the capability to get rid of the mood lighting and brighten up your salon even more, such as after hours to ensure thorough cleaning, for painting touch-ups, or when servicing furniture and equipment.

Lighting for Beauty

Natural light is the best for applying makeup and choosing hair color. However, it's not usually available throughout an entire salon. When choosing lighting, you'll want to replicate natural light as much as possible. Here are some goals for lighting for beauty:

- The light needs to be bright, yet diffuse.
- It must not cast shadows on the face.
- It must not have too much of a tint. Fluorescents are a no-no, with their harsh, blue-green color.
- Incandescent lights, especially softly colored bulbs, are good.
- Many small bulbs are better than one big one.
- For makeup artists, it's good to have some lights on dimmers, to see how the makeup looks in the different light conditions that the client might encounter once she walks out the door.
- Do not fully illuminate and flood an area with light; use only directional spotlights, lighted mirrors, or sconces to cast the right amount of light. Dark paint can be used in combination with lighting patterns for dramatic effects.

Natural Light

Natural lighting is the light that shines through the windows of your store from the sun. This is the broadest possible spectrum. It's provides "warm" lighting tones and, hey, it comes free of charge! A large window can bring a nice feeling into a salon. In fact, a retail store designer may suggest using natural light as a means of showing off your retail products. However, there are many obstacles and issues with natural light.

For instance:

- A huge bank of windows can allow in a lot of heat and even create an unpleasant greenhouse effect inside. Consider UV-blocking tinting for the glass on the windows or light, diffusing shades that also block UV light. These will protect the interior of your salon from the heat and damage that comes with long-term sun exposure.
- Available daylight tends to change in intensity throughout the day, with the weather, and during each season.
- Window space must also be used for displaying products to the passerby.
- Interior salons or ones that are inside a mall may not have any windows to the outside.
- Your salon will be open during times when it's dark outside.

Because it's free, you definitely want to find a way to bring in natural light. Don't block off all your windows. All I'm suggesting is, given the challenges and obstacles of natural light, it's best to have a "backup" lighting scheme.

Setting Up Your Salon's Lighting

One issue you must resolve early in your design and space planning process is adequate electricity, not only for the functional operations of the salon, but also the lighting. In an older building, this may mean updating the breaker box to add more breakers. It probably means adding outlets. But, it could mean that you need some serious services from a licensed electrician to run more wiring for the fixtures you'd like to install.

There are many lighting resources available to retail store owners. Most people get the bulk of the information from local lighting stores. These stores have salespeople who are well versed in setting up stores or at least guiding you to make the right decisions when choosing your store's retail lighting.

I recommend hiring a lighting professional if your electrician or architect cannot assist you with the lighting design for your retail store. Many lighting stores have lighting designers who will help you for free if you buy your fixtures from them. Also, most electric supply stores will be able to assist you or recommend someone to help with your project. Your lighting scheme will be made up of task, ambient, and directional lighting:

- The task lighting will be lights directed at the reception desk or the styling chair for maximum visibility in a defined area.
- The ambient lighting can vary according to style but should provide enough light so that everyone can move about the salon.
- The directional lighting will put spotlights on retail displays and possibly art or signage.

Lighting Fixtures & Bulb Types

Your lighting scheme will include a combination of fixtures and light bulbs. The fixtures you'll choose from serve different lighting purposes, as do the light bulbs you choose for your fixtures.

Lighting Fixtures

The lighting fixtures you choose have both design and functional components. The fixtures will enhance the characteristics of the style that you have chosen for your salon. In addition, they'll serve some type of function. They may light up the entrance, showcase products, allow service providers to see while working on clients, and more. For an introduction to the different types of fixtures, you can go to Lowes or Home Depot. Home Depot has some great Buyer's Guides, including one that covers all ceiling lighting. However, I've also provided some information below for how the fixtures would be used in a salon environment.

Track—These give off a really pretty starlight effect. Track lighting is also good to show off a specific area. You may be highlighting retail displays that have high-selling items or have a track light highlighting the name of your salon. One downside of track lighting is that they throw off a high amount of heat and, if used in the styling area, may cause stylists and customers to feel uncomfortable. They also burn out quickly if kept on for long periods of time.

Recessed—No matter what size your store is, you must always consider your electric bill. If your retail store or salon is located in a mall, you may be required to be open the same hours as the mall, which is seven days a week and as much as fourteen-hour days. Your electric bill could be outlandish if you don't choose the right lighting. Since you often have to install a large number of lights at a retail location, look into energy-efficient fixtures. Recessed fixtures sit within the ceilings of the store while standard fixtures hang and are sometimes adjustable. Energy efficient light fixtures contain lamps that use less energy compared to standard lighting options.

Chandeliers—Great for a grand entrance of a salon. If you have the space and the height, using a chandelier will make any entrance elegant and certainly make your salon quite different from others in the area. They tend to be expensive, so finding one that fits your budget may be a tough task. It may to go to a thrift store or antique shop to find one that best fits your salon entrance.

Sconces—Sconces add such a nice touch and soften any room. These are used in hallways in many spas or treatment rooms. They give off the feeling of elegance yet softness, making the guest relax and feel welcome in any room. They're also used to make a room look formal. Formal is good as long as you are not dressing up a room too much. Sconces can be put on dimmers, so if you're looking to darken a room these do work well. You'll also find that sconces fit into most anyone's budget for lighting.

Spotlights—Useful if you plan to feature certain items or have a display case you want to use in a specific area of the salon for hot new items or sale items. For these areas, spotlights can be very effective. A spotlight is an ideal way to draw attention to specific items or an area. The spotlight shines from the ceiling or wall toward its target. You can also install task or accent lighting, which puts a smaller spotlight on certain items on your selling floor, like items on a shelf or inside a cabinet.

Floor Lights—Floor lights are used in many spas hallways and in treatment rooms to set the mood and heighten the ambiance of a room. They are also used as a safety feature if the spa's hallways are not the bright, due to dimmed lights. Putting lights in the floor is not cheap and they are a pain to change once they blow out. It may sound like a good idea in the planning stage, but most salons and spas that do have them, wish they hadn't installed them in the first place.

Task Lights—Tasks lights are very effective in many areas of a salon or spa treatment room or a utility room. They are simply called task lights because they are used for a specific task, such as to hang over a color-mixing area, where light is extremely important, or next to a computer terminal to see exactly what your receptionist may be ringing up or giving as change. They can be turned on and off when needed and are usually placed exactly where the task is being performed.

Lamps—Lamps are not used in many salons. You may find them in some treatment rooms in salons or spas, as necessary tools for a specific treatment, but usually lamps tend to get in the way and may be dangerous if knocked over or left on when the salon is closed. There are so many better methods for lighting today. Lamps are not what I recommend in the salon environment.

Candlelight—They don't have enough lumens to be very effective in a salon; but candles are the softest, most flattering light and can make a place feel cozy and natural. If that's the kind of feeling you'd like in your salon, place them in a safe place, away from flammables, and never leave them unattended while lit.

Types of Light Bulbs

Lights come in different colors and intensities. Getting a little familiar with the types of lights you might use goes a long way toward that first lighting design session with your designers, contractors, and lighting specialists. You can find great info on the types of light bulbs through an internet search. The guides for light bulbs available through Lowes and the lighting shopping center at Home Depot can help make quick work of your research and education. In addition, here's an introduction to the different types of light bulbs and some tips about using them in your salon:

Fluorescent—These are tubes filled with mercury that give off a very bright light. Because of their brightness, they are great for cleaning. They do NOT, however, belong in the styling area during business hours because they are harsh and unflattering. The spent bulbs also have to be disposed of very carefully, since mercury is highly toxic.

Incandescent—These are the most common bulbs. They come in various colors. The "soft" bulb can be flattering.

Halogen—These bulbs are sometimes used in spotlights. They tend to be expensive and their intensity fades with time. However, most salons use a combination of incandescent and halogen bulbs to create a lighting "tone," that's bright enough, soft enough, and broad enough to also be clear, accurate, and flattering.

Compact Fluorescent Lights (CFLs)—These are required in some cities. They are considered to be wide spectrum and economical (in the long run). Like fluorescents, they can be a little harsh. So, read the label and make sure they are "corrected" to 2700 to 3000K, to best match the softness of the incandescent light bulb.

Specialty Bulbs—Can vary in size, shape, and color. Colored spots can be directed at design features for dramatic effect.

Light Emitting Diodes (LEDs)—These can be another economical way to light specific areas of the salon. They have a long life.

They come in a variety of color temperatures. They offer natural-looking light, which can bring out the best in virtually all retail products. LED's have been praised by many interior designers for providing the most authentic looking light, and you will find that neutral white LED's can provide the closest mirror to what an item would look like under bright, natural sunlight. Some municipalities require a certain number of LEDs in new construction.

Lighting Maintenance

The lighting in your retail will slowly get worse over time. It may not be discernable, but once you clean and or replace your bulbs, you will immediately notice a big difference. Keeping a schedule for maintaining, cleaning, or replacing the lights will keep your lighting at peak performance.

Improving Your Lighting System: Easy as 1, 2, 3

1. **Clean Them**—Lamps and luminaries, like any other surface, collect dust and dirt over time. When these lamp surfaces become dirty, they lose the luster and intensity of the light that they give off. They are working harder to give off the light they would normally give when clean. They become overheated and draw more energy, despite giving off lower levels of light. To properly clean your fixtures follow these guidelines:

   • Make sure your lights are off.
   • If you're using a ladder, set it to the side of the fixtures, do not set it directly underneath a florescent bulb or light fixture. These can easily come crashing down when loosened. If you're standing to the side, you'll be out of danger.

Warning! Do not use water or wet cloths on any bulbs or fluorescents! Electricity and water do not mix! You may cause the bulb to blow up or, even worse, get yourself electrocuted!

2. **Replace the Bulb**—Bulbs lose their lumens with age and stop working as efficiently during the latter stage of their lives. I recommend group replacement, which involves replacing all the bulbs at the same time, before burnout. This will guarantee the light levels in your salon are as close to ideal as possible.
3. **Replace the fixture**—You may have inherited the lighting fixtures when you took over the space for your salon. Unfortunately, you may be stuck with what was already in the space, because the fixtures were attached to the ceiling or walls and the cost would have been too great to replace them. The good news is the lighting industry has come a long way in the past few years. The lamp efficiency and brightness has increased dramatically. By replacing one lamp type with a more efficient version, you'll enhance the light and also reduce your overall energy costs. So, it might be worth it to put together a long-term budget for replacing your fixtures.

Wrap It Up—Consider these crucial spaces in your salon and their specific needs when you're rethinking the lighting plan:

1. Entrance: Doorway, front desk, and waiting area
2. Retail area
3. Service area
4. Color and dispensary area
5. Behind-the-scenes or utility area

22

The Importance of Retail Lighting

Growing your retail business takes so many different babysteps toward success. The location you choose to open your store, the display cases you purchase to show of your products, the trained and confident salespeople you and your clients can trust, and—yes, of course—the products you choose to sell, all have an effect.

There is so much that can happen to drive business away on a daily basis. The weather, a broken water main in the street that diverts traffic from your store, or an unhappy employee who is turning off your customers from buying your products, and the biggest thing in today's world: The economy. These are are impossible to control, simply acts of God, but there is certainly one thing you can do to make sure your clients see the very best aspects of the products you sell. You can let there be light in your retail area, and you can make it good.

Maintaining and growing a retail business means always showing off the best aspects of your products. Whether you sell shampoo, diamonds, or doughnuts, you want your customers to see your products cast in the best light. The way you display them and the lighting you choose will set your store apart from the competitor down the street.

Most small retail stores forget the signigance that lighting plays when attracting customers and stimulating them to buy. Have you thought about the importance of lighting when building your store? Most business owners get wrapped up in the fixtures that hold the product, but ignore the lighting that actually allows your customers see what you're selling.

Why Lighting Is So Important

The first question that comes to mind is, why do you need good light to run your business? Most store owners will agree without light it would be nearly impossible to run any type of business, but how much and why is it so important? Common sense tells us light is an integral part of a retail environment. The problem is most of us think that if we can flick a switch and the lights turn on, we are open for business. That isn't necessarily the case; most of us take lighting for granted.

The exception is jewelry stores. Have you ever seen a jewelry store that wasn't lit up like the night sky on the Fourth of July, spotlights shining so the diamonds and rubies glitter? No way. Jewelry retailers pay more attention to lighting than to anything else, so next time you walk by a bling shop, stop in and see how lighting is really done. And okay, you can try on a few things while you're there! Why not? Point is, high-end and big-name jewelry stores sometimes have specific lighting designers select the types of lights and plan the placement, in order to make those jewels twinkle. Light is the life-blood of the jewelry business, but it's no less important to the salon retail space.

I know, I totally understand you're consumed with the everyday duties of managing the salon, the employees, marketing, ordering inventory, not to mention dealing with customers. The thought of becoming a lighting specialist never crossed your mind when you had the idea of opening your retail store.

The key with lighting is you do not have to have a PhD; just a little knowledge will go a long way. Non-technical people make lighting decisions every day. The trick is to know enough to make the right decisions. These decisions will improve employee productivity, retail sales, safety and security, identification and yes your bottom line.

Problems of Inadequate Lighting

- Consumers have a difficult time with colors. They will pass up a purchase if they cannot decide if the color at your store is the one they will get at home.
- Customers need to be able to read the fine print and ingredients.
- Customers need to see the price of an item.
- Employees may mismark an item or SKU number in dim light.
- Employees may not realize stock is out, so won't order new products, or may misplace items or put them in the wrong spot.
- Employees will take longer finding items that are in a stock room without adequate light—leaving customers stranded at the register.

- Employees may undercharge or overcharge your customers due to inadequate lighting at the point of checkout.
- Safety is always a concern, inside your store and out, so you must have adequate lighting to prevent accidents and also discourage crime around your salon.

Setting Up Your Retail Lighting

When setting up your retail store, everything matters, from your choice of flooring to your display stands. One issue that you must prioritize when first designing your location is setting up your store for lighting. I recommend hiring a lighting professional, if your electrician, architect, or interior decorator doesn't have direct experience with lighting design for retail. Most electrical supply stores will be able to assist you or recommend a professional to help with your project.

Spotlights—If you plan to feature certain items or have a display case you want to use in a specific area of the salon for hot new items or sale items, spot lights can be very effective. A spotlight is an ideal way to draw attention to these specific items or area. The spotlight shines from the ceiling or wall toward its target. You can also install task or accent lighting, which puts a smaller spotlight on certail items on your selling floor, like items on a shelf or inside a cabinet.

LED Lighting—LED lighting fixtures offer a much more natural-looking light, which can bring out the best in virtually any retail products. LED's have been praised by many interiors designers for providing the most authentic-looking light, and neutral white LED's give off the closest approximation to natural light, so customers can see what an item would look like under bright sunlight. When you want your customers to see the most intricate details of your retail items, the best light to show of these products is the LED light. LEDs simply cannot be beaten. Impressions matter greatly, and choosing the right fixtures can make all the difference.

Energy-Efficient Lighting

Your electric bill will always be cause for concern. No one wants to waste money. Your location has so much more influence on your electric bill than your decision to turn lights off at night to save a little. Your electric bill could be devastating if you don't choose the right lighting and make the best use of your lighting resources. Since you often have to install a large number of lights at a retail location, look into energy-efficient fixtures.

Recessed Fixtures—These are the most popular and sit within the ceilings of the store, while standard fixtures hang and are sometimes adjustable. Often these fixtures take energy-efficient bulbs, which use less energy compared to standard lighting options and can save on the power bill.

Natural Light—Natural lighting is, of course, the light that shines through the windows of your store from the sun or other lighting sources outside. This usually doesn't require anything; you simply make it a point to open the shades or curtains on all the windows each day, to take advantage of the natural outside lights. Natural light is a great supplement to your artificial lighting. A retail store designer or a lighting pro will always suggest using natural light to show off your products, but as I mentioned briefly before, in most cases, there are obstacles, such as being located inside a mall or otherwise away from outside light. Or you may have windows that get direct sunlight, so you will have to adjust the blinds or shades periodically. Still, short of cutting a skylight in your ceiling, it's a good idea to take as many steps as possible to get some natural light into your salon. It's good for business and healthy for the body, too.

The bottom line is that lighting makes a big difference in any retail outlet. Whether you are looking to move products or budget goods, the right lighting makes all the difference in the world. Investing in the correct lighting while designing your retail area is the most cost-effective way to approach successful retailing.

Basic Maintenance Goes a Long Way

As I talked about in the previous chapter, improving your lighting system can be as easy as replacing the bulb, or as complex as hiring a lighting designer and construction company to completely restructure your lighting system. You may have inherited lamps and light fixtures that are old, inefficient, or not the ideal kind of light for retail lighting. However, you can mitigate the problems these fixtures cause by exchanging the bulbs for more energy-efficient styles, keeping them clean, and regularly changing all the bulbs in the retail area as a group. This will guarantee the light levels in your retail area remain in top form at all times.

23

When It's Time for a Facelift, Think Big!
(Or Small)

When you're in the retail salon business, the question you periodically have to ask yourself is: When is the right time to remodel? You have tried to wait out the recession. Maybe your thought was when your last child finished college, the financial focus could switch from child back to salon, or when you made the last payment on the loan you took out to open the salon. The old adage says timing is everything, but picking the right time is not that easy. Maybe right now, things are really tight.

The commonly agreed standard in fashion-focused industries like the cosmetology industry is a major facelift is necessary every five to seven years, to keep your salon fresh and distinctive looking. I always look up at the ceiling; if those ceiling panels are yellow and stained from water damage, it's time!

It also may not be apparent to you, but your customers and

staff notice when things get shabby. Even if no one is saying a word, that doesn't mean they don't notice. You need your staff and clients to like everything about their environment. A quick, inexpensive salon makeover can make everyone happier.

Once you decide on going for the remodel, you can plan on spending $20-$50 a square foot, and a month's time, for a project that includes floor coverings, paint, and new salon fixtures. The salon fixtures take as long as 8 to 14 weeks alone for delivery. That can climb to $90 a square foot, and two to four months of construction, for a complete, top-to-bottom redo. For those of you current salon owners, who might not get the rule of cost based on the square footage, let me give you some examples that will be easy to follow, based on the numbers above.

Example: Salon square footage 1150 X $20 a square foot construction, paint, furniture remodel 1150 x 20 = $23,000 total remodel cost.
Example: Salon square footage 2300 X $50 a square foot construction, paint, furniture remodel. 2300 x 50 = $115,000 total remodel cost.

Depending on the size of your salon, a simple calculation based on square-footage numbers (info you can easily find in your lease agreement) should give you an overall price per square foot, to create your budget for the extent of your remodel.

It's definitely time to remodel if it's been five to seven years since you last did anything major to the salon. That's a long enough time in today's retail environment, especially when you consider Internet retailers often change their look one or more times every year.

The investment can pay off. Surveys have shown sales can

increase from 10% for partial remodels to anywhere from 15% to 40% for full remodels! In planning the job, it's a good idea to shoot for recouping your investment in two- to three-years' time.

While the thought of investing in a remodel can be overwhelming, don't let your fears get the best of you. If things are slow, use this time to focus on your salon remodel and a new image for your business. Perhaps you bought this book because you were already considering a remodel of your current salon. Or, you may revisit this chapter once your salon has been open for a few years and is in need of a new look.

Remodel Your Salon & Change Your Image

Over time everything deteriorates. The building you are in may need upgrades. The services you offer may need additions. The décor you choose ten years ago was on the razor's edge then, but now it's tired and out of fashion.

The marketing of your salon, the budgeting process, and how you manage customers and staff have to adapt for your business survival. You can't expect your business to thrive without changing and evolving in appearance, too.

The current appearance of your salon may be dated, tired, and even dirty to your clients, and guess what, when your clients aren't happy, neither is your staff. There is nothing tackier than a front desk with chips, or delamination with tape holding the Formica together, the same goes for your styling stations.

Your staff expects you to keep the salon fresh, clean, and fashion-focused, with the newest trends that they see on TV and in the magazines. This is not only hair we're talking about; paint colors, furniture, flooring, and lighting, it all keeps evolving. What's hot today is out in the cold tomorrow.

The salon industry has always been tied into the most current trends in fashion and design. Your salon must evolve as well or it will die a slow, tired, outdated death.

Once your salon reaches a certain point, it may be too late for a quick, inexpensive rehab. The longer you wait to make changes the more it will cost you in construction and improvements to catch up to your competition. So, ask yourself:

- What do I like most about how my salon currently looks and functions?
- What do I dislike about my salon, as it currently looks and functions?
- Am I happy with the flow?
- Are there areas that are cramped?
- Are there areas where service, sales, or revenue opportunities are impeded?
- Has my client demographic changed? Am I looking to change the style to better match my clientele and a niche that has developed since I first opened my business?
- Am I remodeling on a tight budget?
- Am I planning a major remodel?

As you know, there are different levels of "remodeling" that have differing budgets and may involve the following types of changes:

Design or Layout/Floor Plan—Look at your current salon. Does something in the original layout feel like it just isn't working? For example, the styling area or the color area may not be what you expected and the space may feel too closed off, or the waiting area is too cramped, the shampoo area is too tight, and the dryer chairs jut out and keep tripping people.

Appearance/Décor—After a while, you'll start to notice the dings, scratches, and scuffs. You'll want to take care of those right away and bring your décor up to the current trends. If you can, switch up the color palette to go along with what you are seeing in future stores and home décor magazines. Changes might include painting, new accessories, new light fixtures, new towels, new pictures, adding crown moulding, etc. Or the salon might just need a deep cleaning.

Functionality—When you discover that your current salon layout impedes workflow and is disruptive to providing services, then you definitely need to look at some changes. Sometimes some simple rearranging can do the trick, but sometimes you need to work in a "mini" construction project to get things working better for you and your staff. Taking down a wall, opening a room you're not utilyzing, dramatically changes the look of your salon. Open space is in. The behind-closed-doors look is out!

Focus—As trends change, you might need to change the focus of the salon. For example, a salon that is big on hair-color services really should have a color bar or lab. If your color services are booming, explore whether it's time to showcase those services even more. Think about the space and how to rearrange or rebuild to get the results you want.

Rearrangement—This can be as simple as moving things around to create a sense of interest. Retail displays on wheels can make it easy to do some simple rearranging. But, maybe it's a matter of changing shelves out or moving some of your more "mobile" service stations to different areas.

Replacement—Take a look at what needs to be replaced. Lighting, flooring, mats, carpeting, fixtures, furniture, equipment, etc. If it's looking worn out, then it's time to replace it.

Expansion—When you want to add more services and increase your staff, you'll have to look at expanding your salon. Of course, the most affordable way to do this is to keep your existing space pretty much intact, but just add on. But, if this will put the integrity of the floor plan at risk for awkward flow or poor sightlines, then I would recommend a full remodel.

If your existing furniture and equipment is in good shape, you might be able to just add on to what you already have. If it's worn out, then you should work with your furniture/equipment company on any buy-back options they offer, or list your items on Craigslist or another online site, to at least get something to go toward new equipment purchases.

Describe Your Remodel Project

What changes do you want to make and why are they important to the success of your business? Think about this in terms of big picture as well as small details.

Aspect	Desirable Changes
Design or layout/floor plan	
Appearance/décor	
Functionality	
Focus	
Rearrangement	
Replacement	
Expansion	

Remodel Considerations—Now that you have described what you'd like to do for your remodel, take a moment to review these questions. This section lays out the foundation and factors that will influence how much to spend on your build-out, décor, and/or new salon furniture and equipment.

Budget

- What is your budget?
- What is the overall financial impact of the remodel?
- How do you figure out what you want to spend?
- How do you set an appropriate budget?

We all want the best, but most of us have champagne tastes on a beer budget, maybe even a tap-water budget. Your list of needs and wants may exceed your ability to foot the bill. While the cost of the renovation will vary due to many different things, like how extensive the remodel is and what type of furniture and equipment you choose, you still have to establish a budget.

Deciding on your budget will have you looking at some critical information. Generally, it depends on your demographics, how much you charge for services, and what type of clients your salon attracts. You also need to know what you can afford as a monthly payment, if financing is needed. You should factor in what you already have put aside in cash for the project.

Cost

- How much will it cost?
- How much will it cost to move a wall, rip out the old floor, and buy all new furniture and equipment?
- What should you expect to spend?

Breaking it down to the simplest terms, the cost is a function of the materials you will need for your build-out, the duration (number of days) that the salon will be closed, the labor for the contractors to complete the work, and the new equipment you will be purchasing.

ROI (Return on Investment)

- How long should I expect it to take before all this pays me back?
- How can I maximize my return on investment?
- How do I know if my investment is going to pay off?
- Is there any tax benefit if I lease the new equipment?

There is a particular rule for return on investment in remodeling your salon business. Statistics show that normally you can expect an increase of business of about 20% in the first year of your remodel. This increase would come from new clients that have never visited your salon before the remodel.

Your current staff and existing clients will have the benefit of working at and visiting the hottest salon in the area. The fact that you are keeping your current clientele and not losing staff to competitors down the street is a big factor you have to weigh when you calculate your overall return on investment.

What's Your Budget?

There are many ways to change a look of a salon, so the cost does not have to be in the tens of thousands. Whether your budget is $1,000, $10,000, or $100,000, business will increase most significantly within the first year of the remodel. Keep in mind the changes you make keep your salon looking fresh and ahead of the competition. Your clients will appreciate it and so will your staff.

Let's walk through two different "remodel" scenarios together:

- Remodeling Your Salon on a Shoestring
- A "Big" Remodel or Renovation of Your Salon

Remodeling Your Salon on a Shoestring

If you're working on a tight budget, then most of your efforts will be around freshening up what you already have. It will involve some basic and easy tasks, such as cleaning, which you can do on your own and with your staff; or, you can hire a commercial cleaning service.

Other changes that can still be done affordably involve replacing or painting ceiling tiles and repainting the walls and trim. Again, you can do this on your own to really save money or you can hire a commercial painting service to get the job done. Most of the work for these types of changes can be done before or after hours or on days when the salon is normally closed. Let's review the most affordable "remodeling" options for a tight-budget, quick fix-me-up remodel, or should I say, facelift.

Mr. Clean—The best way to make your salon look fresh and give it a new look is with a deep clean. Roll up your sleeves, put on a fresh set of gloves, and get down to business. I suggest you periodically hire a commercial cleaning service, though—whether it's once or twice a year or even once a quarter. They will get into every corner of your business and wipe away years of grime. This will give your salon a fresh appearance that your clients will notice, and will be a breath of fresh air to your staff. Plus, a nice, fresh floor waxing will make any salon look new.

- Check out your walls; do they need paint?
- Check out your bathroom. Is your vanity tired? Has your toilet seat come loose and lost its luster?
- Do your ceiling tiles have stains and need a cleaning?
- Are your air conditioning vents dirty and stained?
- Does your floor need re-grouting or a deep cleaning?
- Do your lights need to be changed or replaced?
- Does the chrome on your styling chairs need to be shined? Is the chrome plating pitted?
- Does your front desk need an overhaul?
- Does your entrance door need a coat of paint or a polishing?

It's a Bright Light—Replace every bulb in your salon. Light levels in bulbs and florescent bulbs tend to be less bright or give off a yellowish glare after a couple of years. Changing your bulbs will brighten up the way everything in your salon looks. Light brings life! For more information, check back in, "A Bright Idea: Lighting for the Whole Salon."

Bring in New Products—Changing your salon doesn't always have to be with a paint brush and a hammer. By bringing in new products, you are showing your customers you are committed to the beauty industry by introducing them to cutting-edge beauty products. You may have to add some new displays or shelving to showcase your new product line.

Look Up—If your ceiling is dirty or has water stains, either give it a coat of paint or change out the stained ceiling tiles. You really think your clients want to look up and see a water-stained ceiling or caked-on dust while getting their hair shampooed? Eeew, no. This is a sign of true neglect in a salon.

Your Door to Success—The first and last thing your staff and clients see when walking into your salon is your front door. Your front door should always be clean. If it is wood, give it a fresh coat of paint. If it's metal, break out the polish and shine it up. If it's fully glass, you may want to put your name, logo, and hours on the door. This is an inexpensive way to make a noticeable change.

Painting—What is the one thing that can instantly and affordably change the look and appearance of your salon? The answer is new, fresh paint. The best part about painting is that you don't always have to hire a professional to do the work. Most of us are capable of painting. It's usually easy to find family, friends, and maybe a few employees to assist. Bribe everyone with pizza!

Consider changing the color scheme. Changing the colors will give you and your clients the greatest sense of immediate change and satisfaction.

Re-Accessorize—In addition to a new paint color, new art on the walls or accessories in the lobby can give the feeling of change in an instant. You can find nearly anything on Craigslist these days, including framed prints or artwork, vases for a few flowers, or crazy little accent pieces to freshen the look. A discount home store or online home accessories retailer can also provide fun options. A lot of salons are finding plenty of things they like at Ikea and similar places. A change in the color of your towels or the pattern of your capes and aprons can also add a little freshness to the atmosphere of the salon. Even small changes help.

Managing Your Budget-Friendly Project—Even smaller projects need to be managed to get the results that you expect and the return on your investment.

- Establish your budget and timeline (see chart that follows).
- Secure help from staff and/or contractors.
- If you will pay your staff an hourly rate for the project, let them know how much.
- Let staff and/or contractors know the hours when the project will be performed and the timeline for completing the project.
- Get contractor quotes (if applicable).
- Manage your staff/contractors and results of the project.

Affordable Remodel Options

	Needed renovations	Timeline	Cost of materials/ Supplies	Labor costs/ Contractor fees
Cleaning				
Lighting				
New Product Line				
Ceilings				
Walls				
Doorway/ Entrance				

Accessories				
Totals				

Renovating Your Salon - A "Big" Remodel

A big remodel will mimic the original build-out of your salon. Over the next several pages, you'll find helpful guides for each of the steps, so that you can manage your remodel project. Running a project like this while your store is open for business can be tricky. I'll give you sample timelines that have minimal impact on your salon's operating hours and help you juggle permit requirements and the work of multiple contractors.

- Establish your budget and overall timeline (start/finish dates).
- Hire a designer/architect to draw up a floorplan and blueprints.
- Get contractor quotes (if applicable).
- Inform your clients
- Get permits (if applicable).
- Schedule the work.
- Clear the area to be remodeled.
- Complete the work.

Step 1. Establish Your Budget and Overall Timeline, Including Start and Finish Dates

Following is a chart with a sample of some of the types of costs you may incur for your remodel. By completing it, you'll get a full break-down of the costs for what you want to do. It's a good guideline to start seeing how much money you can expect to spend and whether you can afford to do everything you've identified in the remodeling project.

Remodel Budget Worksheet

	Demolition Costs	Materials Cost	Furniture or Equipment Costs	Labor/ Installation Costs
Plumbing				
Electrical				
Drywall				
Painting				
Flooring				
Shampoo units				
Shampoo cabinet				
Styling chairs				
Styling stations				
Dryer chairs				
Color stations				

Color chairs				
Color lab				
Dispensary				
Manicure stations				
Pedicure chairs				
Makeup unit				
Reception desk				
Reception furniture				
Retail displays				
Stools				
Window treatment				
Signage				
Computer				
Telephone				
Other				
Other				

TOTALS				

Estimates: _____

Permits: _____

Architect's Plans: _____

DESIRED START DATE: _____

DESIRED FINISH DATE: _____

Labor Rates/Installation Costs

These costs will help you estimate your construction budget. Prices will vary depending on the city or state.

Contractor's Rates and Installation Costs

(Note: All prices are rough averages and vary by city and state, and from professional to professional. You can't expect to pay Arkansas prices in New York City, so shop around for estimates.)

Plumbers: $30–$75 per hour

Usually a plumber will give a quote on the entire project. They may work by the hour if it is a simple project.

These prices do not reflect any changes in your plumbing, such as adding another sink or moving all the hot and cold water lines over to accommodate another sink unit.

General Contractors: $150–$300 per day

General contractors work by the entire project. Their pay per day can vary based on the magnitude of the project.

Electricians: $65–$85 per hour
• Standard outlet (120 volt) = $100 each

- Heavy-duty outlets (220-240 volts) = $100 each
- Grounded outlets = $120 each
- Upgrading electrical panel (adding circuit, running conduit, installing receptacle) = $650
- New circuit in electrical panel = $185 each

Rates for before or after regular business hours & weekends may be higher, so be sure to ask.

Drywallers: $20–$30 per hour
Usually they will give price on the entire sheetrock taping project. The contractor also should arrange this service.

Painters: $15–$20 per hour
Painters usually will give you a price per job. They may price the work by the day or by the hour, if it's not a big project.

Flooring Installers: $15–$30 per hour
Flooring installers get paid by the job. It may be arranged through the place you buy the floor or your contractor. They work on a price per square foot.

Furniture/Equipment Installation Times and Rates

Wall sink (cabinet installed by others)
1½ hours, including mounting the bracket
$100/unit

Freestanding backwash sink
4 hours on average with bolting the unit to the floor
$250/unit

Pedicure Unit
3 hours to install and assemble
$250/unit

Color lab sink or dispensary sink
1½ hours to install
$175/sink

Facial room sink installation
1 ½ hours to install
$150/sink

Bathroom fixtures installation
Usually ½ day. If it is a toilet and double vanity.
$400

Overall Timeline—A "big" remodel can be done over a four-to-five day period, closing either late Friday or Saturday afternoon and opening up on Thursday for business. All you need is good coordination and good subcontractors who are committed to getting your project done and your salon reopened in a timely manner.

Step 2. Hire a Designer/Architect to Draw Up Floorplan and Blueprints

To find out the costs of this endeavor, I recommend you bring in a specialist in the industry. Several companies specialize in salon layouts and salon furniture. They need to come to the salon, see what you want to change, and discuss the look you want to create. You'll pay a design fee; but I highly recommend it. They have the expertise to give advice on prioritizing the remodeling steps.

Step 3. Get Contractor Quotes

For extensive changes/reconstruction, you'll need to hire contractors. But, every situation is different and it depends on how much remodeling you want to do. If you are just replacing the salon furniture, your installation/labor costs should be minimal. You may only want to paint and change the floor. For this type of work, you may not need a general contractor, but just one or two contractors that you hire independently for the work. How do you know they are charging a fair price? I always recommend the following steps to assess costs:

- Bring in a contractor and get a complete price on everything you want to do.
- Bring in separate subcontractors: a plumber, electrician, floor specialist, and a drywall team to get separate prices on your projects. My rule of thumb is to bring in two to three tradesmen from the same field and have them bid on the same work. Have a complete checklist to hand to them for the bid. Let them know that it might be weekend work or in the evenings, so they price it accordingly. There may be a crew of two to three or just one. Get a complete price without the hourly breakdown. There are always some unforeseen situations, so having a package deal is in your favor.
- Compare bids. If you have three bids and two are about the same and one is considerably lower, there's reason to be concerned. You may be tempted to choose the lowest-bidding contractor, but be careful! That one either did not include something or did not charge enough for labor. There also could be hidden costs he didn't mention. Alternately, that contractor might be the type who's spread very thin, so your remodel

wouldn't be finished in a timely fashion. I would check all the bidding contractors' references and recent work. See if they finished on time and on budget.

Step 4. Inform Your Clients

Put up a sign well in advance to let your clients know you are closing briefly for remodeling. It is also good to show the new design and some of the new furniture on a presentation board; this will excite the clients and staff. Several of your staff will give their opinions on the furniture, their likes and dislikes. Be diplomatic, but remember, this is your business and it's what YOU want to do. Book your last appointment early Saturday afternoon and have your staff ready.

Step 5. Get Permits, If Applicable

If your salon is in operation, it is important to coordinate the remodel so you don't lose any business. If the job is large and permits are needed for the renovation, it's recommended you do your remodel in stages.

For example, in changing your shampoo sinks, you need to pull out the old shampoo unit and cabinets, change the plumbing pipes, and install the new units. It's usually a two-day process. Once it's all done, then it's time to get the plumbing inspector in your city into the salon for inspection. Hopefully the inspector will pass the plumbing work. If not, you can't use the sinks and won't be able to open until it is satisfactory to the inspector and is compliant to all county or city codes.

That's just one inspection! What if you are trying to coordinate several inspections? It gets trickier. In this case, you're hiring a general contractor and it's his responsibility to make sure everything is done on time. The key is to tell him your priorities and let him coordinate these tasks with his subcontractors. Timing is everything.

Step 6. Schedule the Work

Hopefully, you decided to consult a professional in the industry to help guide you with the layout and installation of any new furniture and equipment. Just before the work begins, I recommend a group meeting with all the subcontractors, your designer, and anyone else involved. Have all of the drawings and specifications on hand for all to review and ask questions. Coordinate a schedule so everyone is on the same path and understands the process.

When possible, having the furniture and/or equipment on location is helpful so that everyone can see exactly what will be involved. I've included some sample schedules for projects that include plumbing and electrical. Plus, here are some tips for scheduling projects that involve drywall work.

Plumbing Work—The Process

Working on the shampoo area? Without shampoo sinks, your salon cannot function. You have to be efficient and work with a structured timeline for any makeovers or remodels to this area, because without this department, your salon can't reopen.

For work in this area, it is important to have all of your furniture on-hand or have your equipment supplier deliver for Saturday evening or Sunday morning. You probably will pay a premium for this service. That's life! Don't scrimp on this part.

First, you must tear out the old cabinets and sink units. If you are remodeling the dispensary and any pedicure units, all of this must be taken out as well. Then, the installation begins. Use the schedule below to plan any plumbing work.

Sample installation times, when closing Saturday night and re-opening Tuesday morning:

Three-sink shampoo cabinet	4 hours
Sink hook-up	1-3 hours/sink

Note: A freestanding sink unit with a chair usually takes the longest. Each must be bolted to the floor securely, which is the responsibility of the plumber. If he's a "one-man band," it could take a day and a half for him to secure and install three units, so be prepared.

Scheduling:

- A few weeks before the work, call for a plumbing inspection with the city or county for Monday afternoon.
- On Friday, deliver all new furniture concerning plumbing. If you don't have the room, go ahead and pay the premium to get it delivered on Sunday morning. It depends on your space.
- On Saturday—early evening—demolish all plumbing needed for the change.
- On Sunday morning, bring in your cabinet company to install all furniture concerning plumbing.
- Mid-Sunday morning, have your plumber come in and start prep work on all plumbing fixtures.
- By noon Monday, the plumber finishes and you should be ready for the inspector.

- By Tuesday morning, you will have passed inspection and re-opened your salon.

Electrical Work—The Process

Scheduling: If you don't plan your electric properly, you will have circuit breakers tripping when stylists are in the middle of providing services to their clients. You can only run so many appliances on one circuit before it overloads and trips.

To avoid this problem, bring in an electrician and ask for advice. If you are changing the styling stations, show him the new design. In many cases, the electrical may be in the wrong spot and has to be moved.

Ask your salon-design specialist to lay out your new stations with the current electrical setup in mind. You might not have to make any changes if you can work with what is already there and how it is currently wired.

Unless the salon owner is knowledgeable in electrical systems, the installation of outlets is *not* a "Do-It-Yourself" project, meaning: If you are not a former electrician who became a salon owner, don't touch the wiring! This is particularly true if new circuits need to be added to the fuse panel. Installation should only be done by a professionally licensed electrician. Please don't electrocute yourself trying to nickel and dime your project!

Closing Friday evening and reopening Tuesday morning:
Note: I recommend you close on Saturday because of the unusual amount of electrical work and coordination for this process.

- A few weeks before, call for an inspection for Monday afternoon.

- If possible, order delivery of all furniture that requires electrical work for inspection on Friday. If there is no room in the salon for this, have it delivered on Saturday.
- Friday evening, demolish all old cabinets and furniture concerning electrical wiring.
- Start installing furniture Saturday and finish either that day or Sunday.
- Electrician comes in Saturday afternoon to start working and to make sure he has the right supplies to handle the job.
- Electrician works on all new connections, moving whatever electrical is needed and reconnecting all outlets.
- Work is finished by noon Monday and inspector approves and signs off on permits.
- Open on Tuesday.

Drywall Work: The Process

The work may get done after hours when the salon is closed or during a few hours every evening. It all depends on how extensive the work is. Two things you must be aware of concerning permits when working on partitions or building rooms:

- The room or partition can only be built on one side and cannot be closed until you have approval from the framing inspector.
- If there is any electrical or plumbing going in the wall, you will need a "rough" inspection before you close up the other side.

Once these inspections are done, you can close up the wall and finish the room or partition. You might be able to handle all of this while you are open—it all depends on the scope of the work. Strategize the best approach with your contractor.

Timing is everything when you're moving walls. There really isn't a schedule to follow because each salon is different. I would really urge relying on your contractor to make sure he organizers this type of work, based on the days you can rearrange schedules or close early. Sunday and Monday are usually the best.

Step 7. Clear the Area to be Remodeled

In order for the contractors to complete the project, they'll need the work area cleared. If you are replacing work stations, then the furniture will need to be emptied out:

- Have boxes for each staff member to clean out their station. Have them take the box home or store it somewhere on the premises out of the way.
- Have the front desk team do the same process and clean out the front desk. Also, mark the boxes for all your retail and try to keep it organized for when you restock the shelves later.
- While your staff members pack up their stations, bring in your computer person—your own guru or a representative from the company you bought the system from—to unhook and pack your credit card processor and computer system, so they can reinstall it when ready and not misplace any cables or wires.

Step 8. Complete the Project

- Tear out all unwanted furniture, cabinets, chairs, pedicure units—whatever you're remodeling—and have your salon furniture company or "buyers" pick it up. Try to clear the space as much as possible, so your installers or contractors are not tripping over each other or the junked furniture.
- For the tear-out, your electrician and plumber will need to be

When You Need to Make a Change

there to unhook the existing sinks and any existing electrical that may be attached to the old cabinets.

- Your plumber and electrician will start modifying plumbing or electrical for the new equipment.
- At the same time, bring in all of the new furniture for assembly/installation. Try to work on any assembly of furniture items in places that are not in the way of the plumber or electrician.
- Coordinate with the subcontractors on hooking everything up.
- Once everything is installed, call your staff to set up their stations or department.
- Call your computer person to hook up your system and credit card terminal.
- As everything is being set up, you can finish any light assembly work, such as building the styling chairs or dryer chairs. These items are very simple to put together.
- Set up your retail, clean, and get ready to open in the morning.

Selling Your Old Furniture & Equipment

Your old furniture and equipment may have some value. You may be able to work out a trade-in deal with the salon furniture and equipment company to help offset the cost of your new furniture. If not, try selling it yourself by putting ads on Craigslist. com or eBay classifieds. Get rid of it at any price. If you don't trade it in or sell it, you need to haul it away and that will cost hundreds of dollars.

Recommended Selling Prices for Used Furniture

The prices in the following chart are meant to be guidelines for you; prices for used furniture and equipment can vary widely.

Remember, it's in your best interest to give buyers a good price as long as they're willing to pick up the furniture on your schedule and timeline.

Item	Price Range
Styling chair (depending on make, model, and condition)	$25–50
Dryer chair	$35–50
Reception desk—small (4 to 5 feet long)	$50–100
Reception desk—large	$100–500
Shampoo sinks (fiberglass)	$25
Shampoo sinks (marble/porcelain)	$50–75
Shampoo chairs	$25
Freestanding sink units	$50–100
Freestanding sink units (European or expensive when new)	$100–300
Styling stations (simple)	$10–25
Styling stations (freestanding/custom units)	$50–200
Nail tables	$25–50
Nail stools	$10
Pedicure unit (base model)	$50–100
Pedicure unit (motorized unit)	$250–500
Facial tables (standard style)	$25–75
Facial tables (hydraulic or electric style)	$100–500
Skin care unit	$100–300
Reception chairs	$10–50
Retail units	$25–300
Mirrors	$10–25
Dispensary cabinets	Anything!

Wrap Up: Things to Remember When Starting Your Remodeling Project

- If money is needed from your banker, work out all details before you think about starting your remodel project.
- Let customers know about what's going on and what to expect.
- If you have a plan for a new design and layout, frame and display it for all to see.
- Plan for delays. Your project may or may not totally fall victim to Murphy's Law, but anticipate delays.
- Box all things that may be in the way of contractors and furniture/equipment installers, or that could get ruined, like retail.
- Plan all of your clients' appointments around work schedules.
- Plan the major construction or your new equipment installation during the evening or when you are closed over the weekend.

24

Remodeling Your Bread and Butter

More than likely, you decided to become a salon owner because of your talents behind the chair. Without a doubt, the service area is the bread and butter for your salon. It's the reason why you have clients and the reason why you decided to own a salon, for better or worse.

Your clients are coming to your salon for their beauty treatments. Of course, that can include a new hair style, a manicure or pedicure, a facial, a massage, or any combination of services. Why not make it an experience that is worthy of telling their friends all about, that's worthy of returning for again and again?

If the experience at your salon has grown worn and samey, it's probably time to think about the way your bread-and-butter area is set up, and consider a remodel if there's a long list of improvements you need to make.

Setting up the experience they'll have starts with the design of this main stage area. Your clients and your staff will spend most of their time in this area. It's where the magic happens. So, it has to be perfect and has to:

- Be comfortable for clients and staff
- Convey your brand
- Showcase your salon's services and retail products
- Be memorable
- Efficiently use available space
- Provide ample space for productivity

Let's take a look at each department within the service area.

The Styling Department

Feeling comfortable in this space is very important to clients—they want relaxation, maybe a little luxury, roominess, and a place for their belongings. With those considerations in mind, let's look at the different types of stations and equipment needs for the styling area.

Wall Stations—The minimum space for a wall station, from center-to-center, is 4' 6". That gives ample space for each stylist to work and does not waste any space. Salon owners have used as much as 6' for each station, because of the station design, but when considering revenue potential, adding another foot and a half to each station means that you miss out on being able to add two more stations, which is missed revenue opportunity. I recommend the biggest spread from center-to-center be no more than 5'. Any more than that is wasted space.

Freestanding Stations—These should be no wider than 36" and as narrow as possible. Most of the storage space needs to be located on the sides of the units, with a small shelf in front where the mirror is located. The dimensions for most units are 36" wide and 30" to 36" deep. If you add chairs on each side, the unit takes up 12' of depth.

One thing that needs to be considered when discussing a freestanding unit is the walkway space around the unit where the stylist is working. This is usually a main traffic area. So, it's advisable to add another 3' to each side for traffic flow. The overall depth of the station, including traffic, is 18'. It can change by the way you angle the station, but you won't know until you space-plan the complete salon.

Be aware that you need to hook electrical to the freestanding station, which will either come from the floor or the ceiling. Either one can be expensive and must be researched while designing your remodel.

Potential added expenses and design challenges for freestanding stations:

- If you have a concrete floor and no basement, you will need to cut the concrete to run wiring.
- Exposed wires from the ceiling are unattractive and may not get proper electrical approval.
- You may have to upgrade your electrical panel.
- You may need more lights to give proper lighting to each freestanding station because there is not as much "borrowed" lighting as you would get from wall-mounted stations.

Styling Chairs

- **Chair Containing Round or 5-Star Bottom Base**—The overall dimensions are 24" by 24" around. Weight varies from chair to chair. A good quality chair usually has a weight of 60lbs. or more.
- **Round Base**—More stability, with weight and diameter a factor. For cleaning, it's ideal that it be moveable, because a ring develops from hair buildup around the base bottom.
- **Five-Star Base**—Less stability and easier for a client to tip it over when putting weight on the footrest. Easier to clean by taking a hair blower and blowing out hair underneath the chair.
- **Chair with a U-Shaped Footrest**—This footrest is shaped like a U and has been in the industry for many years. Clients tend to trip over it when getting off the chair.
- **Chair with a T-Shaped Footrest**—This footrest was developed about thirty years ago in Europe. It's a much better design for clients.
- **Styling Chair with No Footrest**—Most of the time, you will see this chair in Europe or Asia, and they typically have a floor-mounted footrest for the client. They do not work for the U.S. market because in America the stylists like to turn the chairs to different positions, whereas in Europe, the stylist works around the chair. I don't recommend going with this style.

Shampoo Sinks

One change-up from traditional salon designs or floor plans is that the shampoo sinks are no longer stuck in the back. This part of the salon is now considered a profit center, showcasing products the clients can buy. With freestanding shampoo units, you can give your salon a dramatic look and make it attractive and visible. Use the number of stations to determine the quantity of sinks (shown in the following chart).

Sink Guideline

Number of styling stations	Number of sinks needed
1	1
2–5	2
6–9	3
10–13	4
14–18	5

These guidelines do not include the sinks for a separate color department. You should use the same formula for calculating the number of sinks, if you have a separate color department.

Note: When purchasing freestanding units, be aware of the type of fittings supplied for hookup. Many of the fixtures are metric and don't fit easily to American pipe fittings. You'll have to get adapters and it could be a time-consuming, aggravating project.

Freestanding Backwash Shampoo Sinks—These units are usually spaced 30" apart from the center of each drain. Doing so gives a six-inch space between sinks. There are many ways to design how these sinks are situated, but you always need at least 30" of clearance behind them for the shampoo person to wash the client.

The general rule is that freestanding units are placed at least 54" from the wall. You can also design the shampoo units to have a gap in between for shampooing from the side. In this case, the plumbing needs to be 48", or 4' on center.

Sinks that Allow Washing from Behind the Sink Only, or from Behind AND from the Side—To install freestanding sinks, the floor will usually need to be cut for waste and waterline installation, which can be expensive. If you have a location with a basement, then floor cutting is not an issue and it's very easy to move pipes and put the sinks where you desire. However, I recommend you insulate the hot water lines in the basement. Usually, they are exposed and may be too far away from the hot water heater to maintain desirable water temperatures.

Wall-Mounted Shampoo Sinks—Generally, each wall-mounted sink takes up 4' of space. So, if you have three sinks, it will take up 12' of wall space. You can go a little smaller, but be very careful with spacing for wall-mounted sinks. You need to account for 2' for the sink itself, plus another 2' between each sink. Anything less than will make it difficult to get in between the shampoo sinks without bumping into the next sink over when shampooing a client. For most wall-mounted sinks, the waste and waterlines can be installed in the wall, which can be a cost savings. Whenever possible, your wall-mounted sinks should share a wall with your utility area, which will keep the water heater close to the sinks.

Each location is different. Review these options with your designer and architect for the design option that is best for your design features, budget, and space.

Hair Dryers with Chairs

Location of salon	Recommendation
Near retirement communities	1 dryer per 2 styling chairs
Progressive coloring salon	1 dryer per 4 styling chairs

Note: A dryer on wheels can be useful for overflow.

Pedicure Department

Now, it's time to talk about the pedicure department. Can you believe over 40 companies manufacture all the different types of pedicure units? It can be very confusing. So, I'll break down each style unit so you can choose the best one for your space.

Option 1—Chair with a separate footbath. It's the most basic style and the footbath ranges from $30 to $100, depending on the functions. The water must be filled and emptied by the pedicurist for each service. No plumbing is required and the "plastic" footbath needs to be sanitized after each use.

Option 2—Chair with a separate footbath that has a built-in pump. This unit is portable and can be put into a closet and taken out for a single use. After use, the unit needs to be brought (on wheels) over to a sink or toilet to discharge the dirty water, which is done by the pump in the unit. The price range for this type of unit is $775–$1100.

Option 3—Pedicure unit built like a "shoeshine" bench. These do look very good and have a nice, cozy appeal. They can be built three different ways:

- Least expensive: unit with a portable footbath (described in 1)
- Unit with a regular sink (kitchen style) which gives the pedicurist water for filling and draining. It's built into the unit, flush mounted.

- Unit with a whirlpool sink which looks like a kitchen sink, but contains the whirlpool capability with pumps built underneath the unit.

All of these built-in units look great and usually match the rest of the salon in color. But, they all have the same common problem—the unit has no height adjustments.

The benches are designed to sit at a certain height. Many companies design the bench for an average person 5' 6" tall. Let's say you have a male client who is 6' 4" tall. When he sits in the unit, his knees are up to his chest! A woman who is 4' 11" will need to slide down just to reach the bowl. Usually, you will need to supply pillows to prop that person up and the pedicure becomes an uncomfortable experience.

Some of these units come with nice options. The bottom line is that, if they have no height adjustment, they won't work well for all of your clients. Another possible issue is that these units are made of wood (mostly plywood) and laminate. If water splashes on the surface and it's not sealed properly, then the wood will swell and cause delamination. The price range for these units start at $800 for the base model and can go up to $4,000 for all the bells and whistles.

Option 4—Pedicure unit with a piped whirlpool system. This type unit has been in the industry for a long time. What I mean by "piped" is that tubes are running inside the unit and water gets pushed through the pipes by a motor. Then, the water is blown through jets that create a whirlpool action.

Warning! Over the last ten years, some states have outlawed this type. The reason is that after you use the unit, a small amount of water is left in the tubes inside of the unit. There is no way to sanitize the unit completely by flushing the system. If the unit is not used, the water—even though it's a small amount—builds bacteria, a natural process.

Once the unit is used again, bacteria can wash back up and attack the client, creating a rash or open sores. There are documented cases of this and I do *not* recommend this style unit. If you do buy this system, carry good insurance and be prepared for trouble! The unit ranges from $1300–$2000.

Option 5—Pedicure unit with a "pipeless" whirlpool system. A "pipeless" pedicure unit has all the same functions as the "piped" unit, except it has no pipe. It contains a motor that's built behind a fan and it's mounted inside a tub that's covered by a plate. The plate protects you from any injury. The motor turns the fan, which creates a whirlpool and, after use, you take the cover off and sanitize it, so there's no issue of bacteria.

There are many types of units and the price range begins at $1800 and goes up to $12,000. My recommendation is that you buy this item from an established dealer. With a lot of these units, you'll have problems, regardless of how expensive. You want to choose a reputable company so that you can count on them to still be in business when a problem arises with the unit.

Manicure Area

Now that we've finished the pedicure area, let's talk about the manicure or nail department. What I've found in my experience is that most commissioned "nail techs" make, on average, about 70% commission. Once you buy supplies and handle all of the booking, you're lucky to make 10%. Salons have manicurists as a service for their clients, so they come to their salon for more services, stay at their salon longer, and create more loyalty.

My suggestion is that you rent the manicure area out and let your renters buy their own supplies. If you compare the numbers, you'll make more money renting this department out, and suffer a lot fewer headaches.

For creating a manicure area, the normal size of a table is 48" long by 18" wide. The height of the table should be 30" and I suggest you position manicure tables with the short side against a wall, spaced 6' apart. That gives enough room for the client and nail tech to sit comfortably.

Facial/Massage Department

The last department to talk about is the facial/massage suite you might put into your salon. If you already have tiny alcoves or rooms somewhere in the back, at least 7' by 12', you're set. The only other considerations are the cost of adding a sink and cabinets (in the ballpark of figures already discussed for the shampoo area), a massage table, plus a different decorating scheme.

The ambiance of these rooms might need to be totally different from the rest of the salon. For instance, the light fixtures will need to be compatible with dimmer bulbs, to soften the lighting, and you'll have to choose deeper paint colors and upholstery, in lieu of the cheetah prints you might love. The furniture is the place where your budget could be trimmed or could balloon, since a massage table or facial chair could cost you anywhere from $100 to $3,000, depending on what style you want.

You could also add a shower to the massage and facial suite. Considering the cost involved, though, it would be like adding another bathroom.

25

Roll Up Your Sleeves, You Are Under Construction

Building your business has not been an easy task, I'm sure. You took the steps necessary, and that final leap of faith, to become an entrepreneur, so kudos to you! I understand, though, that eventually the daily burdens will start to weigh you down. No different than the construction project in your salon's space. This is probably the phase in the life-cycle of your salon when you're going to feel the most powerless, but it doesn't have to be that way. The fact is, there will be plenty of times and occasions you just have to jump in, like you did when you opened your business. Yes, I know, there's only so much you can do to help move the construction project along—you don't know how to install flooring or trim a window!—but you can still roll up your sleeves and get your hands dirty.

Maybe you just had a French manicure and you don't want

to literally get your hands all messed up, and some of the things you may end up doing will be uncomfortable for you. Get over it, rearrange your schedule with your clients, get some help from family, friends, and even some of your staff, and get some of the basic things done you would normally have to hire someone to do. Doing some basic projects yourself can save you money and leave you with new skills and accomplishments to be proud of!

You know you're the most creative person in the world; that's why you decided on cosmetology as a career, but perhaps handy-work was never one of your strong suits. Maybe you just can't get your head around how you could possibly assist with moving your project along, but it's not as hard as you think! I'm going to show you some simple ways for you to be instrumental in keeping your project on track, staying out of the pros' way, and still saving yourself time and money, without losing your existing clients along the way.

How to Get Started

You've decided to take the bull by the horns and jump into your salon construction project, wonderful! But you've never done this before and have no idea where to start. You haven't decided on equipment, your design is still just "almost finished," and construction is about to get underway. What to do?

The following are the daily functions that can keep your project on task, plus save you time and money along the way.

Don't Work Without a Design—Some projects require an architect, some an interior designer, but sometimes a talented builder will get your aesthetic and help you come up with a good plan. Whatever you do, don't start a startup or a remodel without a detailed floor plan. A lot of elements interact in a space; put them all on paper and you'll catch problems before they're built into the remodel. You may be able to build a functional space without a plan, but if you want a functional *and* beautiful space, hire a designer.

Schedules Rule (Your Life)—Make a schedule with your contractor, once you decide on one. Make sure you both agree with the schedule and this becomes part of not only your contractor's routine, but yours as well. It's important to have an agreed-upon schedule for any project, no matter how small or what this person is doing for you in the salon.

The schedule keeps your contractor accountable for getting the finished product completed by the end date. Remember, each day you're not open, you're paying rent, electric, gas, and insurance on a space you're not making any money in. You also have to worry about employees abandoning ship before they can start back up in your beautiful new salon, due to delays on your opening date. Stylists get finicky quickly if you're not open when you say you will be, especially if they're new hires. You most likely will have to start the hiring process all over again.

Don't Delay Decisions—If you want things to go well in your new and improved salon, the best thing to do is make every single decision *before* work starts. A good builder can talk you through the list of situations that might come up on your job, but decisions about situations aren't usually what cause delays.

Instead, most of the issues are related to decisions about things like paint, trim, and salon furniture selections. These may seem minor, but when your backwash units are two weeks late because you couldn't decide which one you wanted in time, plumbers have to be rescheduled, or a wall has to be moved because you choose a different style that's just a few inches bigger than the original. You can see how a molehill will turn into a mountain, with a week's delay on a five-week project.

Visit the Job Site Daily—Make sure your contractor is there and check who's working on your salon. Drop in by surprise, so you can see if your plumber, electrician, sheetrock person, and contractor himself are onsite actually doing some work. Outta sight, outta mind. If you're not around, most likely your contractor won't be, either. Unfortunately, this isn't always realistic—and if you've worked with or know your contractor personally, this may not be necessary—but visiting as often as possible won't hurt.

Unscheduled visits will show you mean business and will ensure things get done. If no one is there, call your contractor and ask why. No need to stay long; just make a presence. If you don't show up, but instead just call and check in, you have no idea if anything is getting done or if anyone showed up to work. You lose a day if people don't show up. If you come by at the end of the contractor's work day, make a checklist of what was and wasn't done. Call your contractor when you get home and discuss the next day's plan. This will also keep your contractor's payment schedule in check. Why pay him if the job isn't getting done according to the schedule you agreed upon and signed?

Demo the Old and Bring in the New—Most contractors don't get offended if you decide to do any needed demolition yourself before the construction starts. If you take down a few walls or rip up an old floor yourself, it can save you a good amount of money. Keep in mind, if you've never done anything like this before, it's probably going to take you three times longer than your contractor.

You also have to be careful when you're taking down a wall that an electrical cable, a gasline, or the roof doesn't come down with it! Double and triple check with your contractor or architect that the wall you want to remove isn't a load-bearing wall and can come down without weakening the structure of the building.

It's a really good idea to buy some thick gloves and a hard-hat if you're taking down walls, plus a crowbar, so you don't hurt your back. This type of work is not easy. If you come across plumbing lines or electrical wires in the wall you're releasing all your stress on, don't touch them, work around them. Leave the hard stuff for the professionals.

Clean Up—Taking on the task of some of the job site cleanup doesn't cost you anything and keeps the job from becoming a mess. This should be done by the general contractor, but usually the electricians, sheetrock guys, and plumbers make a mess quickly. A messy job means a messy workspace. It's hard for workers to do a good job when they're stepping on everyone's garbage and leftover materials.

This is a thankless job, but if you can stop by once or twice a day, put on your gloves, and clean up, it helps everyone. It sure does help the building process keep moving along.

Take Out the Trash—Taking away the trash can save you thousands of dollars and save your contractor some valuable time. The first thing you need to do is borrow a pickup truck or rent a truck or trailer. The average rental for the day is minimal compared to what your contractor may charge you for trash removal.

Here's something to consider before you take on garbage duty, though: After you rent the truck, where do you take the trash? There's a good reason your contractor wanted to charge you to take it away. You'll need to call your local municipality or search their Web site to find out where you can unload building materials. The last thing you want is find out, once you drive up to your local dump, is that your municipality puts your trash in the "we don't want it" category because they feel it's hazardous!

Making the List and Checking It Twice—Many salon owners (or should I say people in general?) take the contractor's word about pricing as cast in stone. If you're buying flooring, lighting, bathroom fixtures, whatever, check online to see if the price your contractor is charging is in the ballpark of where it needs to be.

It's not unusual for a contractor to pad the number he quotes as the purchase price of material, claiming 120% to 125% of the price, then passing the increase on to you. If *he* knows *you* know what he paid for the materials, you may be able to negotiate a better price. Keep the money in your own pocket!

That being said, make sure you're comparing apples to apples before you come after your contractor yelling "Cheater!" Did you find the exact model of sink faucet the contractor is ordering, or did you find a different brand that's less expensive in general, and probably lower quality? Let your contractor know you're on the ball without coming across as accusatory or unreasonable; after all, you have to work with this guy!

On-Time Delivery—Most equipment manufacturers work with the person who's ordering and paying for the equipment. Most likely that's you. Salon equipment is usually delivered 6 to 8 weeks from the day you place your order and pay your deposit. If you are ordering any custom equipment or special furniture from overseas, it could be as long as 12 to 14 weeks, sometimes longer. It's up to you to schedule all equipment so your contractor knows when he needs the electrician, plumber, and carpenters on the job to install your beautiful new salon equipment.

Delivery dates are essential if you want to run an on-time project. Remember, your contractor most likely has other projects, so do the electrician and plumber. Perfect set up for the domino effect, if the delivery date changes for your salon equipment! The minute you find out a change has occurred, get on the phone with your contractor, so he can get the ball rolling on organizing his team to meet the truck when your equipment arrives. FYI: Your equipment will have to be paid in full before it leaves the manufacturer's warehouse! No ifs, ands, or buts. That's the policy in the beauty industry.

Equipment Delivery—So, you have the schedule for your beautiful new furniture. Everyone is lined up for the install. Job done, right? Wrong. Nine out of ten times, you'll have a curb-side delivery. Okay…so, what does that mean? It means exactly that. The truck driver will drop your very expensive furniture at the curb. He doesn't care if it's raining, snowing, or even if you're there to keep it from getting stolen. He gets paid to deliver; that's it. He drops the goods and goes. Ouch!

Most people don't realize how heavy salon equipment is, until they have to move it. This usually seems to happen when no one is there to help. Styling chairs get delivered in boxes the size of washing machines and can weigh up to 75lbs. or more. Styling stations are made out of plywood or compressed board. I can't even begin to guess what they weigh. Point here is: You'll need help.

In my experience, most electricians and plumbers will not assist moving equipment; it's best to hire a few extra hands the day you expect the equipment delivered. The problem is you just don't know when it's coming. You know the day, not the time.

If you've ever waited for furniture, it's always a pain trying to figure out when it's coming. Promises, promises! Most likely you're going to end up paying your help for the entire day just to keep them there, unless your equipment comes first thing in the morning.

The day before your equipment is delivered, go to a home or hardware store and pick up a few items. This list may seem weird, but you'll understand once your equipment gets dumped at the curb:

- Dolly or flat-bed cart to put under your boxes, to get from the curb to inside the salon.
- Roll of brown construction paper and duct tape. You'll need to cover your equipment once it's in place to protect it from damage from the contractors. It's not uncommon for a tool to drop or a utility knife to slice a new styling chair by accident, while the contractor's crew is rushing to get the job done on time. Better to cover and protect them than have to wait for a new chair or front desk or, worse, a replacement for a broken mirror, due to not preparing for the possiblities, or just being plain lazy.

Construction costs typically are about $60 to $70 per square foot of the size of the space of the construction zone. For example: if your space is 1000 ft^2 and is estimated at $60 per square foot, it could run up to $60,000 for a complete salon project. Keep in mind this is an industry standard. If you've had any kind of construction done, you know that overruns and lack of knowledge on your part can be expensive—making it the riskiest and most costly phase in the life of your salon. You can easily end up 20% to 30% higher than you budgeted, if unforeseen issues come up, or if you don't manage the process and contractors well. If we use the example above, 20% higher than $60,000 is an additional $12,000. I've seen this happen many times. Going over budget is the biggest pitfall when building and starting any business. It can kill you before you even open your doors to the public.

Although many of the things we just went over seem difficult, once you start, the key is just putting your mind to it and getting it done in an organized and methodical fashion. Depending how you tackle it, this may be the best time of your life or the worst. Just buckle down and march through it, because doing so will save you cash and ensure you have an on-time reopening. Imagine how happy and satisfied you're going to be with the work you did, once you're sipping that hard-earned glass of wine at your "Grand Reopening" bash!

26

How You Know It's Time to Move Your Salon

When you decide to do something as huge as move your business, there must always be a good enough reason for pulling up stakes and planting yourself in the next plot of land. For some, it may be one big but simple reason. For others, there are multiple factors. Listed below are the top reasons why businesses move. Where does your salon or spa fit in?

More Space—The most obvious example is your business has grown and is adding staff or additional services. The once-comfortable working space is no longer adequate for everyday business. This is a great problem to have, because it means you're succeeding!

Another reason that crops up most often is the need to merge two businesses. The merging of the two businesses forces the owners to search for space that will establish workable conditions for the combined groups of clients and staff.

Owning Instead of Renting—In many parts of the country, space is at a premium like never before. For many business owners, the time comes when renting is no longer a viable financial option and buying becomes the only sensible thing to do. With rent on the upward trend, buying a place becomes more desirable. Buying eliminates the threat of being squeezed out of your space and ends the cycle of constant rent increases.

Owning the building or space does bring more responsibilities, such as maintenance, finances, and ongoing upkeep. However, the most important benefit you have when you get ready to retire is you can sell the business and property together or separately. It gives you a built-in retirement plan!

Evolving Neighborhoods—As with anything, neighborhoods change and develop. Different circumstances may force you to relocate your salon. The move may be the most important thing you do for your business. If the area is changing for the worse, your clients and staff will only welcome the move into a new environment. Be on the lookout for signs of neighborhood deterioration.

Relocating Near Home and School—Whether you're contemplating a move to another state or just across town, getting your business closer to your family, your children's school, or even closer to the place you want to eventually retire can make great sense in the long run. Long commutes can work out if the increase in profit at the business site and the decrease in living expenses at the home site are great enough, but think of your commute in these terms: every hour you spend on the road is a haircut you didn't perform.

Business Divorce—For better or worse, richer or poorer, the breaking up of a business partnership is a predominant cause of business moves. When business partners split, the owners usually go their separate ways and find a new place to continue daily business. Keep in mind, even if the split is peaceful, clients and staff you thought were loyal may end up on the other side of the street. Any move, no matter how well-planned, will result in some amount of loss of clients and staff.

Upgrading and Investment—As business prospers, many salon owners realize their need and desire to expand their location, or convert their hair salon to a full-service salon offering wellness or spa services. When searching for space, it pays to go a little bigger. If your growth has been on a continual climb, the new space will be inadequate within a short period. Moves are extremely costly, so you do *not* want to do this every other year. When you plan new space, be certain to have some additional square footage for business growth over the short and long term.

Downgrading/Downsizing—Getting ready for retirement or being overwhelmed with managing a large staff may be reason enough to eliminate all those extra rooms and square footage. That's a common reason for businesses to move to a smaller space. The downsizing move has to be carefully planned and skillfully budgeted, though, because your lowered capacity will mean decreased revenue. When you're moving in order to increase space and capacity, you're in essence betting on a corresponding increase in profit. Moving to a smaller space means you have to budget for less revenue still covering the financial hit you took from relocation expenses. Make sure ahead of time the lower rent and bills will make it worth the change.

Mull It Over

Finally, even though you may believe you have adequate reasons to move, I would still caution you this endeavor can be extremely complex and costly. The decision will require outside professionals to assist you with your evolving relocation plans.

On the other hand, moving can be the most rewarding endeavor you accomplish in your business career. A well-planned move can benefit your business venture and revenues, assuring a healthier and more lucrative business down the road, once you're past the headaches—and backaches—of the move itself!

Part Three

What to Do
When Things Are
Going Wrong

27

How You Know Your Business Is In Trouble

It is not uncommon for a small-business owner or manager to wake up in the middle of the night thinking about the business. I'm sure this has happened to you. Your significant other, business partner, family, and friends say you worry too much. This ongoing battle to get a good night's sleep is pretty typical, not to be perceived as a genetic disorder. No need to run to your doctor to get a prescription for sleeping pills!

It's perfectly normal for entrepreneurs to worry about their business. And nowadays, with all the negative news about global economy and generalized nervousness about the slow recovery here at home, that worry is even more understandable.

If sales are relatively normal, the solution may be to focus on the positive and pep-talk yourself out of worrying so much. Hey, remember no one ever said owning or running your own salon would be easy. If you're feeling anxious about your work life, unfortunately this is part of the ups and downs of the business world, and the motion sickness that comes along with them.

How do you know if you truly are worrying for a good reason, though? Your new business doesn't come with a magic crystal ball that can forecast how things are going to turn out. It would be amazing and save many people the heartache and the financial burden of opening, then closing, so many businesses if this crystal ball did actually exist.

However, there are plenty of easily recognizable signs that can show your salon is sinking. Here are a few:

No Detailed Cash-Flow Budget and Projections—Cash flow and profits are not the same thing, and the number-one reason businesses fail—even those with strong potential—is because they run out of cash. Most startup salons, or salons in business fewer than two years, open without a plan and budget. It is essential to know how much cash you have and how much you need to operate your business.

You Are the Only Person Bringing Big Dollars—Businesses that learn to operate without depending on the owner have a chance of success. If you are stuck behind the chair 24/7, how can you grow the business and look for new customers? Smart bosses have standards systems in place to provide leverage for owners and promote growth, without depending on one or two key people.

You've Lost Your Edge in the Marketplace—If you are a me-too business, offering the same services and selling the same retail products as every other salon in your area, you won't last long. You need some sort of edge that matters to your current customers and new client prospects, to keep new faces coming through your doors and the old ones coming back. Your edge can be product education, retail products other salons don't have, operational excellence, superior service, or technology that allows your customers to manage appointments online, buy retail online, and find out what's going on in your salon through your Web site and social media presence.

Your Salon Provides Lousy Customer Service—No business owner ever admits to providing lousy customer service, yet too many businesses do just that. It is crucial to understand your clients' expectations, know the magic moments when you can make or break the clients' experience, measure results, train employees to delight clients, and put in place standards and procedures to assure consistent service.

You Don't Have the Right Salon Team to Succeed—Salons need talent —put the right person in the right seat in the bus and the bus drives. If you don't have a salon training program, good systems in place, salon software, a reward system for top talent, and a recruiting process from a nearby cosmetology academy, your business won't last as long as it otherwise could.

You Never Keep Track of Inventory—Retail means detail, so if you lose track of inventory or continually spend cash on retail you don't need, there's a problem. Also beware if you have a backroom full of products from a year ago you haven't sold, which are collecting dust on your storage shelves. Without a salon software system to keep track of inventory, you will find yourself overspending on products you don't need.

No Clear Direction or Buy-In—You don't have a clear direction for your salon team that every employee understands and embraces? Trouble. If you play favorites with your staff and don't communicate with each of them the same way, your salon is not running on all eight cylinders. It's much more powerful to have a dialogue with employees about where you want to take the company and how you will get there. Embrace what they have to say, learn from each other's mistakes, and communicate effectively daily.

Your Salon's Fixed Costs Are Too High—You opened the salon with too much space. Your intent was that you would grow into the space quickly. Now you have an extremely high rent, property tax is through the roof, and your utilities are killing you. With the economy the way it is—and maybe a recent walk out—you now have a giant space with only a handful of employees. High monthly overhead will kill your business, no matter how hard you try to manage well.

You Have a Bad Attitude—One of the biggest reasons businesses don't last beyond one year is because the owner cared more about ego, status, and maintaining control than about having a successful business. Don't blow this off; I've seen it again and again. Strong business leaders surrender control to top talent, and place greater emphasis on growing business and bottom line results than on their status or ego. You can be the life of the party and center of attention after work; leave your ego at home. If you are lucky enough to have stylists who knows more than you do and are more talented, let them spread their wings and make you money. Take a deep breath, ignore any envy you might feel, and reward them for their service. If you don't, you'll lose them and your business will die.

Cash Goes Out Before Cash Comes In—If you're over-spending on retail products, new gimmicks, image events, and ineffective marketing that require large cash outlays, but you're not seeing any cash inflows, then you are perpetually at a risk of loss. Stop spending hard-earned money on salon *stuff*. The *stuff* will put you out of business.

Your Staff Runs the Show—If your salon team dictates what goes on and how your business is run, you might as well shut your doors today. Running a business means just that. You need to captain the ship, or the ship will sink. Life jackets required; head to shore as soon as you can.

Trouble on the Horizon

These warning signs are pretty easy to spot and quantify, but what about the first small waves in the salon that warn of dangerous waters on the horizon? Some indicators your business is struggling may not be easy to recognize at first. Many of us struggle to see the signs that things are getting bad. Usually, it's our egos that get in the way of perceiving exactly what others already see. Your staff, customers, family, and friends may actually pick up on the vibrations that things are not so good at your place of business before you do.

The first step is that you understand your business may be sinking, so you need an emergency strategy to turn things around and get your ship back on course. Here are some of the first warning signs that trouble is brewing on the horizon:

Customers Don't Seem to be Coming Back—The nightmare scenario for most entrepreneurs is the loss of customers. This should be one of the easiest signs in your salon to read, to take the pulse of your business. Simply put, loss of clients equals less money in your cash drawer at the end of the day. Perhaps a new salon opened around the corner from your place of business. Maybe one of your stylists is scaring away customers with his or her attitude. Possibly your front desk person is miserable and has a hissy fit when someone asks to change an appointment or buy a bottle of shampoo. Whatever the reason, customers aren't coming back. As the owner or manager, it's your responsibility to figure out why and get back on course before it's too late.

What to do? The first step is to find out why your clients are bailing on you. If indeed it's a situation beyond your control, that's one thing, but perhaps the decision to leave was the way your run your business. It's important to understand that when clients leave and don't come back, change is needed before any more clients go the same way. I'll discuss lifejacket client-saving strategies later in this section.

Staff Turnover Is Higher Than Usual—Many times your staff can feel the ship is sinking before you realize you have problems. Your staff may get together when you're not around and do what people do best, dramatize the situation. The what-ifs may start to fly around your shop like a colony of hornets. "What if:

- The salon doesn't pay the rent; will we have a place to work?
- The owner/manager doesn't pay us, how will I pay my bills?
- The supplier doesn't allow us to sell their products because the salon didn't pay the bill?
- My clients find out I work for a deadbeat?
- No one else will hire me because I worked for a salon that went out of business?"

We all know none of this is may be true, or maybe your business is struggling but not to the point of closing, but all it takes is one slip of the tongue and you could start to lose employees or, worse, have a complete walk-out. The problem with the staff knowing you're having business issues is they'll want to jump ship before it goes down. That in itself can exacerbate any other challenges, because finding stylists with a good book of business when your salon is struggling is nearly impossible and if you have to hire any new staff, it will be time-consuming and, yes, expensive.

One possible solution? Connect with staff. A good way to stay on top of employee morale is to hold regular meetings to discuss the good, bad, and the ugly the salon may be going through. Honesty is the key to employee retention. Engaged employees are less likely to quit, especially if their views are respected.

The Fun-Factor Is Dwindling Quickly—When you were planning on opening your business, or found out you were getting promoted to manager, just thinking about your salon put a smile on your face. Everything was fresh and exciting! Fun sounds frivolous, but it's enjoyment and enthusiasm for what we do that makes us successful. If you're not having fun and you find yourself constantly worrying about keeping your doors open, then most likely you're not bringing your best to the venture. This could be a tell-tale sign that, indeed, your company is headed toward trouble.

Here are the sentiments I hear a lot: "I was really excited when I first started my business, but now, you know what? This is more than I bargained for. I made more money working for someone else and spent less time doing it. No bills to worry about, no drama, no late payments, no missed appointments with family. No arguments about money at home."

Not many entrepreneurs have a business that is entertaining, or should I say fun, every day. Yes, it helps, but any good profitable business has its ups and downs. It's not always fun and games. There are always aspects you'll like and aspects of your business you won't like, but an overall sense of satisfaction is important in running a business.

It's true there are entrepreneurs who are at their best during the startup phase. When it comes to the day-in, day-out reality of running the business, they're not as excited and many feel bored. Throw in the difficulty of making ends meet with the daily management duties of running a salon, and, BAM! The "fun" party is over. Been there, done that; get me out of here.

This may be a sign. Call it a wakeup call. What to do? You can consider either selling your salon or taking the less dramatic option of delegating more of those daily duties to your most trusted employee, while you focus on marketing, building business, and enticing new clients to try your salon. These are the fun things that made you happy in the first place, anyway.

Your Business Lacks Focus—Your salon team is full of jacks-of-all-trades but masters-of-none. This can be deadly to your business. Being perceived as okay and not really all that great is a difficult way to maintain and continue to attract new business. Focus on being good at one thing. Color or cuts, it's tough to be great at both. Great athletes may be good at all sports, but usually concentrate on being spectacular at one. Be spectacular and watch your salon business soar.

Your Salon Doesn't Concentrate On Retail—If your salon is not selling retail, then you will not grow your business. Period, end of story. Retail brings back repeat business. Your staff should be educated in retail and understand the products they use and sell. Without this, you will die. But enough with the dire warnings, think about it this way: Retail does not call in sick, have mood swings, fight with its spouse and come to work angry, or continually cause drama and stress in the salon. Retail is your most dependable and loyal money-making sidekick in the salon.

Marketing Is Not a Priority—Your idea of marketing is word of mouth. You felt if you built the nicest salon in town, then people would eventually find out about you, then come in and give your salon a try. But probably, the old expression, "If you build it, they will come," is not working. Often less-deserving salons do better business than the fancy, higher-priced salons because they make marketing a top priority. If your business isn't using at least seven different channels to get visible, then it's at risk.

Your Banker Stops By for a Visit—When you first sat down with your new banker, you were so eager to show off the business plan you had been working on for over a year. You had everything budgeted, down to the last penny. Your business plan was a sure-fire way to put you on the fast track to financial independence and, hopefully, early retirement. Your business plan was so good that the banker was just as excited to lend you the money needed to open your dream salon. Does all this ring a bell?

Fast forward, your salon has been opened a year and what seemed like a fool-proof business plan had a few holes in it. You forgot to plan for a bad economy, a salon opening up around the corner from yours, a walkout with half your staff leaving, or some of your best customers leaving and going to a competitor. If you're started to get behind on loan or mortgage payments, or you're starting to bounce a lot of business checks, be prepared.

Warning signs your banker may be coming to call soon:

- You start putting your personal money into the business to make payroll or rent
- You start using credit cards to pay for your retail order or back bar (this was okay when you were trying to rack up mileage or points, but now you're just paying the minimum payment and your balance keeps growing)
- You start to skip bills at home and bill paying, which has always been a chore, is suddenly something you don't want to do at all (easy not to pay when you have no money!)
- You have depleted your rainy-day fund at home and at work just to make ends meet (needed the money to pay your supplier last month!)
- You start to look for interest-free credit cards, thinking you can use them now and will be okay next year, but begin to use them as a means to pay business and house expenses (things will get better eventually, right?)
- You begin to use one credit card to pay the others balance (no end in sight!)
- Your bounced-check fees begin to rise at your bank (must be the customers' checks, not mine!)
- You have hit your limit at the bank and have balances on your overdraft fees (insufficient funds), on all the bounced checks (can't believe how rotten the service has gotten at the bank after all these years!)
- You blame your accountant for all your problems (can't be my fault)

None of these indicators is a sure sign your business is sinking and you, as the captain of the ship, are going down with it. But any one of them could be a clue that you need to respond quickly to manage a situation before it becomes a real problem. If you're just starting to see these dark clouds appear on the horizon, there may still be time to escape the storm.

What you need to tell yourself: "I'm in trouble! I need to get back in control of this situation!"

If your business model sounds suspiciously like even a few of the listed items above, then this section of the book is for you. *What to Do When Things Are Going Wrong* will help you turn your sinking ship around. We're going to patch the holes, fix the leaks, get your salon ship back in tip-top shape, get your crew ship-shape, and set you, the captain, sailing toward a profitable port. Ready? Set? Let's *Gooooo*!

28

Save My Business!

Here is the million-dollar question, and the reason you've flipped to this page: Is it possible to save your salon business? Maybe you've been in business for a few years now, but things really seem to have taken a turn for the worse. What do you do? The big question you have to ask yourself is, can you survive? The next thing you need to find out quickly is *how* to survive.

Does this sound familiar? Sales are down. Costs are going up. Your landlord wants to raise your rent. A new salon moved in across the street. To make matters worse, you just had a walk-out and lost two of your best money-making stylists. Facing these difficulties, it's no wonder you feel like you're about to have a nervous breakdown! It's overwhelming. What can you do to turn your business around?

I'm going to discuss in detail a few critical steps to take when your salon business is in peril. These business-saving tactics will enable you to quickly implement the *Ready, Set, Go!* strategies to get your ship off the bottom of the ocean, then get it floating, gaining speed, and making money.

However, before you can implement any lifesaving tactics, you have to review the problems that have been plaguing your salon. Take a long, hard look at your business. Try to dissect why your salon may not be as profitable as it once was, which you have some tools to do now, after reading the previous chapter. Maybe the main reason you can easily see is revenue has declined. Look at all the reasons for declining revenue. Do any of these fit your situation?

- Sales in the salon are low and/or declining.
- Customers have left and not come back.
- Your staff members are leaving and you're not able to replace them.
- There is competition in the area you know about.
- There is competition in the area you don't know about yet.
- A traffic pattern has changed in your area, to your detriment.
- The neighborhood is changing and may be in decline.
- The shopping mall where your business is located is declining and losing tenants.
- A new strip mall or shopping location is hotter and your clients are now spending time and money there.
- Buying patterns in your community have shifted.
- Your community has lost a major, city-wide employer.
- You are sick and not able to manage the salon.
- You lack necessary management skills and/or training.
- There is drama and disharmony in your salon.
- Your pricing structure isn't based on your clients' income level.

- The prices in your salon are not high enough to make you money on the services and retail you sell.
- Your salon furniture and fixtures are in disrepair.
- Your salon needs a makeover to look more modern and attractive.
- Your salon is not clean, polished-looking, and inviting to guests.
- Your salon needs a deep cleaning to get rid of built-up grime.
- Your salon needs a paint job to look fresher.
- You don't have salon software to assist with inventory, client retention, payroll, and daily bookkeeping.
- You don't have a bookkeeper or accountant to assist you with paying bills and finding the optimal tax situation.
- You haven't fully utilized your retail salesperson or sales team as a sounding board for helping grow your business, educate your staff, and promote your salon.
- It's been forever since you attended an industry beauty trade show to find out the newest trends, products, and education methods.
- Your staff is not dressing for success or otherwise showing they are leaders in fashion, so their customers don't feel like they're receiving services from the best in the beauty industry.

So, we have gone through a slew of factors that can drive away business. If you answered, "Yes, that's my salon," to any of the items above, you now realize you have some serious problems. But, don't throw in the towel just yet. We need to dig a bit deeper, to see exactly what you can change and where you need to plug holes quickly. In short, we really need to dissect the story behind the story. You can't do much about, "sales are low," but you certainly can do a lot when you find out what your customers and staff want, and what you're doing wrong.

Jot It Down—Make a complete list of all the problems you see or opportunities you haven't taken advantage of. Don't do any editing. If it pops into your head, you're thinking about it, so write it down. The list may end up being a mile long, but at least you are realizing there are some major issues, so you can start to put them in high-priority order to get started. Let's make a plan together and *attack*!

Don't Trust Yourself Alone—The second step is to get some input from a trusted business person. It may be a good idea to have a chat with your accountant, attorney, or a small business consultant. Ask them what they think about your list of problems. What have you overlooked? Have you missed something important? What items shouldn't be listed as problems? What does this person think are the most pressing issues? What fires should you attempt to put out first and where do you go from here?

The idea of going to someone not involved with your salon is that they have no ties to it. They are not emotionally attached and they will give you their honest opinion. That puts them in a good position to help with the plan of attack.

One other major point is they will most likely bring up ideas or problems that never occurred to you. In all honesty, they will come up with ideas and solutions more powerful with quicker results than you are able to, since they have the needed distance.

Put Out the Biggest Fire First—Your to-do list may be as long as you are tall, but you need to address the biggest problems first. Don't try and put out all the fires on the first day. Start with one and try your best to get that one finished, then go to the next. The worst thing you can do is freeze up when you realize you're to-do list is too long. Take a breath and just get started. Rome wasn't built in a day and your problems will be there tomorrow, if you choose to go home and rest in the evening. Working on all your issues at once may leave you in a worse state than you're already in; you may burn yourself out before you have the chance to douse every fire. Remember, if you're still behind the chair, you also have to concentrate on your bread and butter, which is your clients.

Break each problem down into daily action steps and set aside one hour a day to work on them. During the hour, don't answer your business phone, your cell, don't text or tweet or check email. FOCUS on the task at hand! You'll need all your brain power and concentration to take action and get the problem solved.

T.L.C. Needed—When the ship is going down and you're working your tail off to save it, you'll be under tremendous pressure. Not only emotional pressure, but financial pressure as well. Trust me, you will start to get a little cranky. This is a great time to get up earlier than normal and hit the gym or a yoga class. Releasing the stress will not only make you feel better but make you more focused to the task at hand. Even when he was campaigning like crazy in 2008, Barack Obama still hit the gym every morning.

While you're dashing around saving your business, it will be difficult to stay focused. You'll feel compelled to drop what you're currently doing and put out the fire of the day. Unless you have special training as a super hero that will be difficult. Ugh! Why even show up tomorrow? You won't have fun, you won't make money, and it's not healthy for you and your family.

This means you may have to let some business fires burn. There will be damage, your credit may have some hiccups and you may no longer get invited to your landlord's Christmas party. So what? There is nothing you can do about it. You're only human and have the same 24 hours in a day as everyone else. You have to accept the fact it will take time to save your business. No one ever said owning or managing your salon would be easy!

Reality Check

I hate to bring up something no business owner wants to hear, but it's possible your salon business is beyond saving. OMG! Yes, this may be true. You may have done everything possible and depleted every dime of your savings. Maybe your spouse or mate is about to leave you; your kids, friends, and family have had enough, and your health is becoming a big issue.

Before you lose your mind, it may be you just have to give the keys back to your landlord and shut her down. Even Donald Trump has had to do this; why not you? There's absolutely no sense in kicking a dead horse, and there are plenty of other things for you to do with your life and all those aspirations.

Closing up show will not be easy to do. It'll hurt you more than begging for help or asking family or friends for money to keep your business going. The blow to your pride of watching one dream end will be painful, but life will continue. You can pick up and take your clients to another salon. Being back behind the chair with no distractions will be a good thing. You will remember why you went to cosmetology school in the first place.

It will be amazing after a few months that family and friends will like being around you again. You may even have some money in your pocket for a much-needed vacation.

Sometimes, people feel they need permission to admit defeat and retreat. Here, I'm giving you that permission right this minute. Even if you close your beloved business, I guarantee life will go on.

29

Resolving a Major Crisis in the Salon

No one likes to receive a complaint from a client—but complaints are worth their weight in gold, if an organization learns from them and uses the information to improve the client experience. Client complaints can be used to build a better customer experience and turn a dissatisfied client into a raving fan. How your salon team handles the crisis will determine if your salon offers five-star services or handles conflict the way your competitor down the street does, which is poorly.

The key is for the service provider to immediately take action. Make sure that employee asks what would make the client happy and then verify before taking any action. Clients will rarely ask for more than you're prepared to offer, so ask what will make them happy first. Once they've made their suggestions, then verify that, if you are able to provide that remedy, the client will be satisfied. Nothing feels worse than working to resolve an issue, only to find the client is still not happy.

Move quickly to resolution, once a resolution is agreed upon. In fact, a good recovery builds greater customer loyalty than simply delivering as expected, so make sure to use this to your advantage. The exact opposite is true, however, if the customer is "given the runaround," before their problem is handled. A scorned client unhappy with a cut or color is a lose-lose situation, since a badly done women's haircut lasts at least six to eight weeks. That's a long time for someone to simmer about how awful she looks and how bad the service was at your salon. The worst part is this client can quickly go to the internet and start an onslaught of negative publicity on Facebook, Yelp, Twitter, Google Plus, and more about your salon, her service, and how poorly she was treated. Ouch! You'll be catching it from all sides!

Provide the tools needed to resolve salon crises, by giving employees options when dealing with difficult customers or those with an issue the employee can't resolve. Empower your team to take charge if a crisis does arise. For example, if a customer bought an item on clearance, but the store's policy is never to accept returns on clearance items, allow employees to offer the customer a complimentary gift card or similar bonus. While it may not be exactly what the client asks for, it will show appreciation and show them the salon is going out of its way to satisfy them.

Empower employees to handle client complaints themselves. Obviously, there will be a point when a more senior person has to make a decision in dealing with a complaint, but empowering employees to deal with common complaints and issues on their own will go a long way toward creating a more positive client experience and increasing employee engagement. It also helps when a manager or the owner of the salon steps in, to see how they can lend a hand to the employee to resolve a crisis. Showing teamwork is a good approach to resolving an issue. It also shows the customer everyone is interested in resolving an issue and gives the perception that each client is important to you and your team.

There will be times when nothing can be done to satisfy an unhappy customer. At that point, the service provider must simply refer that customer to a manager or the salon's owner. The owner of the salon or manager must present the client with a solution. I wish I could say your clients will behave decently and maturely every time they have a complaint, but that's wishful thinking. Brace yourself for unpleasantness some days. Once you get past the screaming and yelling and inappropriate name calling, figuring out the right resolution takes a little quick thinking. Duck and cover is *not* a solution. The problem will not resolve itself. Provide a solution to create closure. However, before suggesting a solution, here is the sequential order of crucial considerations for creating the best resolution:

1. Determine the future worth of the customer. Don't make the mistake of an inexperienced business owner by assuming the customer is always, always, absolutely, unquestionably right, or by altering your attitude based upon the flac they throw up in your face. All that's important at this point is to quickly assess the future worth of the customer.

2. Ask the client what they want to resolve the matter and if the solution you offer will make them happy. The client's response will indicate whether they are reasonable or not. This will help you further determine the future worth of the client. Are they making unrealistic demands? If so, chances are they are going to add more trouble than value to your business. And if the client *is* being reasonable and has brought up fair points, it

becomes easy for you to give them what they want—creating a more satisfying experience for them.

3. Determine what it's going to cost you to resolve the matter to the client's liking. Weigh the price of the resolution against the future profits they'll bring you. If they are suggesting compensation that seems excessive, look at the bigger picture before you accept or deny their demands.

You're not finished yet. Presenting a solution is not the final step. Once the customer has been satisfied (or you're satisfied with the extent of your solution), there are two more steps to take to minimize recurrence of the issue and the loss to your business:

1. Determine whether the client is right or wrong. Now is the time to assess the client's perception. If the client was wrong, consider what led to their perception and the possibility for other clients to come to the same conclusion. If the client was justified in complaining, giving them closure to the problem is only a temporary, Band-Aid solution. Keep digging down to find out the root of the problem.

2. Implement a corrective action. Create a procedure to both cure the root problem and to implement policies on how to handle similar situations in the future. It will give your employees peace of mind, too, if they have some precedents set for how to handle issues.

If you never have unhappy clients, chances are that you don't have very many clients. Whether the root of their ire is a bad day, or if a bad experience with you truly had the power to ruin their mood, being prepared with these quick steps will only benefit you as you create the best resolutions for your business.

30

An Accountant Can Save Your Business

See if this sounds familiar: You opened a salon because, even as a child, you knew you wanted to be a top hairstylist. You followed your dream through cosmetology school and your first few jobs, and finally opened a salon in your hometown. Dream fulfilled! Now your salon is open and you have the reputation of being the hottest spot in your area, but there's tiny little problem. You're not making money and your finances are a mess. On top of that, you can't get caught up on your taxes.

Okay, so you opened the salon, your salon has the right reputation, and you have everything you always wanted. The problem is that in cosmetology school, you learned the art of hair. You aced it! You're the best stylist around. You know it and you're proud of it. The one thing you know you are *not* good at is accounting. One of your clients tried to teach you Quickbooks. Looked and sounded easy! Quickbooks became Quicklooks, then you never looked at it again! Why pay an accountant or bookkeeper when you can do it yourself, right? NOT! You're falling behind on your bills and the IRS is knocking at your door. What do you do?

If you find yourself making excuses instead of getting caught up on your bills, accounting, and taxes, your business can and will be in trouble before you know it, if it isn't already.

When you owe taxes, the interest adds up quickly. A double-whammy late payment penalty will be charged, too, unless you show a reasonable cause for not paying on time. You can try to tell Uncle Sam that you're too busy to pay your taxes, the dog ate your receipts, or you spilled Redken Color on your check book while doing a client's hair, but none of that is going to get you anywhere.

It's time to accept the fact you need outside help. You need to hire an accountant. Does the thought make you draw back in horror? Big business means big fees, right? Usually, yes, but what about small businesses? Are there any benefits to investing in an accountant's service when you're a small business?

Well, just like there are big salons and smaller ones, there are smaller, one-person accounting firms or firms with a few partners that do a very good job assisting small salons and businesses all over the country. This type of accountancy specializes in supporting smaller, local-community business. You'll also find their fees are tailored to the type of services you require, how many employees you have, and how much money your salon earns. The smaller amount of money flowing in and out of the business means the way it needs to be managed will be that much simpler.

What an accountant can do for you is help you get caught up on bills, turn your ship in the right direction, and keep Uncle Sam from capsizing your business. Sound good? Let's take a look.

Bookkeeping Advice—Keeping track of all the day-to-day transactions allows you to account for the money moving in and out of your salon's business. There are different ways to keep your salon's books, depending on the type and size of your business, and an accountant can advise on which would suit your particular business best. Choosing the right one can save you time and make sure you claim all the expenses possible, so you can to reduce your tax bill. The right accountant can also assist you with getting your taxes due paid on time. If you have a problem doing this yourself, many accountants will be able to offer this service as well, at a small monthly fee.

Solutions: Taxes paid on time, bills paid on time, and more time to concentrate on clients and growing business!

Cash-Flow Advice—If your cash flow stops flowing, what do you do? If you can't manage your cash flow, that can actually put you out of business. How is that possible? Just stop paying your employees on time, or your landlord, and you will quickly get a lesson on how cash flow can sink you. It's all well and good, having a salon full of customers and money coming in, but when it slows down or stops, you need money in your business checking account to pay bills that are due.

An accountant can help you plan properly to check your cash flow, keep up with expenses, manage paying suppliers, and pay employees. He or she will help you spot any problems or slowdowns early enough to give you a chance to head them off, realign your current position, and keep your pipeline of cash steady enough to pay bills on time, and even pay yourself as well.

Solutions: Money to pay bills, happy employees, cash flow for a rainy day.

Personal Financial Advice—Maybe you've been in business for five years and haven't saved a dime. How is that possible? It just seems like every time you want to put some money aside for retirement or for your kids' college fund, something forces you to pump it right back into the salon.

The whole point of being in business is to make a good living from it. An accountant can advise you exactly what you can take from the business and how much money you should be putting back in. They can ensure you get the most from your hard work and allow you to save for your retirement, college for your kids, and anything else down the road.

Solutions: Retirement plan, children's college fund, money in the bank for a rainy day!

Inventory Control—Why buy retail you don't need? Your accountant will be able to run reports, look at your inventory stock, and tell you when to buy. Having products sitting in boxes in your back room or garage waiting to be sold is a sure way to let good operating cash go to waste and leave you short when you need it.

Solutions: Inventory control means you only buy what's needed, leaving you with cash for operating expenses or payroll.

Business Planning—Accountants are involved in many types of business and see them at all stages, from start-ups to long established corporations. Because of this they are able to bring a wealth of experience to look ahead at how your business could develop, and provide guidance on how to manage your financial growth.

Solutions: No more worries for your growing business. Now you have a game plan and guidance along the way.

Getting a "Yes" from Your Banker—You need a loan to get you back on your feet, but the bank wants a personal financial statement and a business plan. Okay, gotcha, but you have no idea on how to fill out either for the bank.

Your accountant does this on a daily basis and will surely put you on the fast track with the bank's loan application and necessary paperwork for your much-needed loan. Your accountant may even have a relationship already with the bank or may be able to suggest a bank that's lending money.

Solutions: You got your crucial loan and now have a relationship with a bank you would never have had, unless you used an accountant.

Tax Planning—Uncle Sam changes the tax regulations all the time, as each budget brings a new round of politically motivated updates. Accountants keep up to date with all these changes and are able to advise you on how these changes may affect your business. New rules may change how much you owe or have to shell out for employees. With this in mind, an accountant can set aside more of your money for these changes.

Either way, you can concentrate on business and not worry about things you can't control and understand. Why waste valuable time on things that can be done by your accountant? Think about it this way: The money you save in interest and penalties for *not* paying taxes will surely cover you monthly or quarterly accounting bill.

Solutions: Taxes paid on time, no fees or penalties, and easy sailing!

Knowing Where You Stand—You don't need a crystal ball to have a clear picture of your financial situation, you only need a good accountant. A clear picture allows you to make good financial decisions when necessary. No need for quick reactions when a sudden bill pops up or you have an emergency that requires you to outlay some hard-earned cash. Making good choices, having a plan, and understanding what your business looks like financially will only help your business grow. When the time comes and you have to make a big financial move, you will be standing on solid ground because your accountant is taking good care of you.

Solutions: Money when needed, ability to focus on your long-term goals, and money put aside for emergencies!

Time Is Money—A huge part of owning a salon is managing time. Time is money and we only have some much time to work in a day. How you work is what makes you money. Working on taxes, payroll, bookkeeping is time consuming. So, do you work on bookkeeping or clients? It's a no-brainer! Do what you do well and leave other things, like accounting, to the specialist. That's what you're paying your accountant for. If you're a top-class stylist and salon owner or manager, you're far better off using your time for that, to bring in more business, than pecking at a calculator, paying bills, or working on balancing your books.

I know you're going to say that money is tight right now and you're struggling as it is. You don't have the extra money for an accountant. However, you really have to think about this investment. It's rare to find the money you spend on the services of an accountant is not more than repaid in the ways they can keep you on the right track, minimize the taxes you pay, and keep you from making costly mistakes.

For all the reasons I talked about, an accountant can help you *make the most* of the money you do make. It might not be that much at the moment, but when you turn this ship around who knows how much it will be? Isn't it better that it stays in your pockets rather than getting frittered away in interest and fees? With a good accountant, you make the most of the money you bring in and free yourself up to make more of it.

31

How to Use Your Salon's Credit Cards as Life Rings

There's no temptation in modern America as universal or as irresistible as overusing credit cards. Maybe you've done it before—almost everyone has—you spend and spend and spend, having a great time and thinking things are going okay. One morning, though, you wake up and find yourself with a balance you can't pay off and no spare cash beyond the minimum monthly payment. OMG, big trouble!

This doesn't have to be your life, though. Credit cards are actually great tools that can save your salon money and enhance your business, if you're super savvy about how you use them. Make your card use count! I'm going to go through the nitty gritty of how to make your business cards work hard for you, and how you can raise—or should I say, bail out?—your credit score.

Golden Rules for Using Cards

Pay Your Bill On Time—Of course this is the most basic rule and should be a no-brainer, but it's worth making this your mantra. Every month you don't pay on time, the bank or store will slap you with a late fee and your rate will jump. That's salon money down the tubes, just because you forgot or the bill got lost in a stack of junk mail.

Set up recurring email reminders in your phone, on your computer, in your online payment system if you have one; you can even be old school and write it on your wall calendar, just get it done! That being said, no one is going to shoot you for being late once if you're a good credit user and pay on time every other time.

It's normal for people to forget a bill once or twice in the life of their card, so call the credit card company, explain that your family medical emergency or your going out of town caused you to miss the bill, and ask if they can waive the fee and forgive the slip-up. You might just get what you ask for, if your payment history is otherwise solid. Just don't abuse this option. Once is enough. Twice, you're pushing it. Every month? You're toast.

Pay the Whole Amount—Very simply, pay in full and you won't pay any interest at all. End of story, happily ever after! Of course this means you can only spend on your credit card what you can back up with cash in the bank. If this were possible for everyone all the time, it would be a miracle. However, this can, should, and must be your goal when using credit cards, since it's the only way to keep all the money you can in your own pocket. Paying interest, in the end, is like donating money to the bank. Do they need donations? Doubtful. Does your salon need the money you and your employees worked hard to earn? *Oh, yes.*

If You Have a Balance, Pay It Down—Okay, so life happens, you had a flood in the salon that cost a ton. You can't pay your whole balance every single month of your life. The next best option is to pay down the balance aggressively. Ignore the minimum payment and pay as much as you possibly can, especially on higher-interest cards.

Remember not all cards are created equal. Some have introductory offers of zero-interest for a few months, some have low interest, and some have interest so high it will murder you. Prioritize paying off the high-interest-rate card first, then the low-rate card, then the card that still has the zero-interest-rate deal attached.

Here's another really motivating reason to pay the maximum you can each month: A high balance doesn't just mean you have to pay more money sooner or later, it's also hurting your company's credit behind your back! For example, let's say you have a Visa card that has a credit limit of $5,000 and you've charged up $4,500 on it, plus your salon American Express card has a $10,000 credit limit and you have a $9,200 balance on it, from beefing up your retail inventory and maybe handling a crisis, like a flood and equipment damage. Those are red flags to the credit bureau. Because the balance is so close to the limit, your credit score is going to start falling, since you look like you're in danger of going over the credit limit.

Juggle Wisely—You know yourself. You've been living with yourself for a long time now, so I have confidence you know if you can handle a lot of credit cards or not. If having five credit cards attached to your business means you're going to spend five times as much, it's time to snip three in half and restrict yourself to two.

But! If you're the type of person who can stay on top of paying bills, here's a really hot tip for using cards like a pro. Your salon's credit score will be healthier if you have five cards that you only charge up 30% or less, than if you have two cards you keep charged up to the limit. It's counter-intuitive, but that's how it works. Think of it this way, if you have five buckets with only a little water in each, it's better than if you have only two buckets and they're already full. There's more room for water in the five.

So if you've been paying your salon's two credit cards diligently, look into adding a third card from a major bank to give you a way to spread your spending and keep each "bucket" less full. Man, oh man, is it going to take self control! If you can do it, though, that third card can raise your credit in the long run. Just don't open a fourth and fifth any time soon!

Note: If you need to get rid of a card, it may not be the best idea to call up the credit card company and cancel the card. It's probably better to pay the balance off completely and just stop using the card often. Once the balance is paid, the card can add to your good credit history, just by hanging around with no balance!

The credit card company may close the account automatically after a few years, but you can keep it active and healthy-looking if you make a small purchase every six to twelve months and pay it off immediately. This is a trick to increasing your credit score, especially when you're in a situation where every point counts, like needing a loan for your business soon. Talk to your banker, though, before you decide whether to cancel or keep a card.

Watch Your Statements Like a Hawk—Banks make mistakes, plus fraud can happen to anyone. If a thief gets your business credit card number and wrecks your salon's credit with fraudulent charges, who do you think is going to suffer? Your business, of course. Even if you recover the funds, think of the wasted time.

Protect your salon and yourself by checking your statements regularly. Not just every month, but once a week! The sooner you catch a mistake or fraudulent charge, the more likely you are to get your money back before your salon's credit is shot.

It's also a good idea to have some sort of fraud protection with your bank. Most credit card companies have good fraud departments, so look at the Terms and Conditions on your card, or call the company and ask, to see how you're protected and what the terms are. Which leads me to my next point.

Read the Fine Print—I know it's not going to be any fun and you'd rather be doing *anything* else, but take the time to read all the Terms and Conditions in fine print on your current cards, and any new cards you want to get for your business. You'll be amazed; there are so many ways for a bank to zing you with fees: annual fees, cash-advance fees, balance-transfer fees, late-payment fees, and fees for charging over your credit limit. And it's not just the fees that you need to understand, but also how your interest for different instruments (like cash advances) is calculated, plus how payments on your balance is going to be allocated, once you send your check to the bank.

If you use a card for a cash-advance (just remember: cash advances are only good for emergencies!), there's going to be a fee for using the cash-advance option, plus the amount you pay on your credit card balance and cash advance together will apply to the lower-interest portion of your bill.

The bank wants more of your interest dollars, so it's going to use your payments for the part of your bill that makes them less money. Reading all the fine print will tell you that critical information! Just think of it as reading the rules of Dodgeball, only here it's Dodge-Fees-and-Interest-Ball.

Check Out Your Credit Score—But not too often! There are three credit-reporting agencies, Experian, Trans Union, and Equifax. You have the right to ask each one for a free credit report once a year, so if you stagger your requests to each of the companies, you can get one every four months. Make sure you're getting credit for all your on-time payments and good stewardship, and no suspicious-looking lines of credit are appearing, which would mean fraud and possible identity theft!

The problem with checking your salon's credit score, though, is that you're not the only one checking it—banks are checking, the credit card company you just applied to is checking—and every query about your credit is noted in your credit score. If too many people are checking too often, it's a red flag to the bureau, because it looks like you're running around asking every bank on the block for credit.

Ask for a Lower Rate or Switch Cards When Necessary—If you're making payments on time, keeping your balances low, and generally being a smart cardholder, it may be time to ask for a lower rate or switch to a lower-rate card. Research what kinds of interest rates other credit card companies are offering; call your company to see if you can get a lower rate, like the one you saw at XYZ card company. If you've never asked before and you haven't earned late fees or overcharged in the past six months, you might just get what you want. Credit card companies want loyal cardholders, so they'll sometimes cut you a break. If you've got a good case for deserving some perks, it never hurts to ask!

By following these guidelines and keeping informed about how you can use credit cards to your salon's advantage, you can be the captain of your credit, just like you're the captain of your salon. The bottom line is to stay alert and stay informed. Learn to choose the right credit cards for your salon's needs and how to leverage the power of those cards to improve your salon's credit score. Chances are good you're going to need a loan for the business someday, or will need to refinance the loan you already have, so keep your spyglass turned toward the horizon, so you can recognize dangers to your salon's credit score, as well as opportunities to sail your credit in a better direction.

32

I'm Losing Customers! Help!

Estimates vary, but most studies suggest that the average small business loses over 25% of its customers each year. Many salon owners assume that their customers are loyal and would never leave. The old rumor in the cosmetology industry is that most women would rather leave their gynecologist than their hairstylist. Okay, enough said, but yes, customers do leave. In your case, it may be more often than before.

Perhaps this is a phenomenon you've noticed: After the first flush of success with your grand opening and all the energy you and your staff had to get started, clients have started to drop off the radar. That client who came in every month for a touch-up of that gorgeous color job you did for her, that young businesswoman who came in for regular blowouts, that gregarious mom who had the best stories about her kids, have they all disappeared?

Many entrepreneurs assume that, once a customer decides to leave, that customer is gone for good; there's nothing the salon can do to lure them back. A customer-service expert will tell you this is a misconception because the cost of wooing lost clients back is lower than the cost of attracting new ones.

Let's assume that you have lost a good number of clients. The experience I've had with hair services is that when a client leaves due to a bad service, bad experience, or whatever the reason, one of the first things he or she does is consult with friends about where they get their haircut or color done. Usually he or she will try a referred salon next.

I can almost guarantee the first time these lost clients try a new stylist, the chemistry will not be there. The clients will end up with something not exactly what they wanted and will wish they hadn't left your salon in the first place. In defense of the new stylist, it usually takes at least two to three consults to get to know a client before he or she can begin to understand their wants and needs. Timing at this point is critical and your window of opportunity to reconnect is now. Don't say it's too late just yet. Here are some different ideas to lure your clients back into your chair and get them spending money again.

Analyze Your Numbers—First, look at your numbers to see by how much exactly your sales are down. You then can get a better handle on how many clients have left, have cut back on their services, or simply aren't coming in much anymore. Once you break down the numbers and loss of services, you can then dissect your customer base by salesperson or customer-support personnel: front-desk staff, colorists, shampooers, nail artists, facials team members, masseuses, etc. You should be able to break down each service area or department to quantify the loss of client base.

Examine Your Losses—Clients don't just up and leave without a reason. The first step to reclaiming them is to determine who they are and why they left. Meet with your staff and explain what's going on. If each stylist has lost a few clients, there may be big-picture problems with the way you're operating your business or the way you're training your staff.

If there's one person, specifically, who is losing the lion's share of the clients, you have your culprit. You might have to consider different measures, like intensive retraining or even dismissal.

But first, let's work on getting the clients back. Deal with the latter problem another day. One big problem at a time.

Your salon staff and customer support people may surprise you with why they say some of their customers left without telling you. You will hear many different reasons why a particular customer left, but those answers may not be correct. Make a note of what your employees say, check the stories against each other, but remember, there are always two sides to every story.

In the salon business, no matter what the issue is, in order to make the clients happy, you have to live with their story. Unless it can damage your business, harm your employees, or put you in jail, the customer is right. Your staff members may not be old enough or experienced enough to understand. Maybe they just don't care; they don't own the salon.

It's up to you to drive home the point and let your staff know the ramifications of not abiding by, "The customer is always right." Obviously, there is a problem that needs fixing, because customers are gone!

Get the Client's Side—The most important step is this one. You have to somehow capture the reason the client decided to leave. There are a few ways to do this, but it's not going to be easy. Sometimes, the last thing a client wants to do is hurt your feelings or get their previous stylist in trouble. On the other hand, sometimes the *first* thing the client wants to do is make trouble for their stylist, especially if they left because the stylist was rude or incompetent. Either way, coming up are some methods to capture this data.

Solicited Dear-John Letter—One method is to design a comment card to send in the mail for the clients to fill out. A card is a lot less confrontational than a phone call or conversation in person, so you might get clients to open up more if you don't put them on the spot.

If you can afford it, make the card self-addressed and stamped, so it won't cost the client money to give you their opinion. Start the message with something like: "We haven't seen you in a while; we miss you!" Then go on to ask a few leading questions to get the client thinking about why they left. Don't forget to add plenty of lines where the client can write their own response. Here's where the information will get juicy and you might find out information you need to put into an action plan, such as your stylist needs more training on color, or your salon looks dingy compared to the new one up the street, or it's too difficult to book appointments.

Phone Call—Asking clients directly why they left can also be effective, if handled delicately. Plan to do this yourself, or else hand the job to very skilled employees who have proven track records with high-quality customer relations.

Call the client at a time that's less likely to be disruptive, like a weekday before the dinner hours of six to eight, or on a Saturday or Sunday, late in the morning. Start the conversation saying that you haven't seen the client in a while and just want to know if everything is okay. Ask a few leading questions, stressing that you are interested in gathering information to improve your salon's service, *not* trying to put the client on the spot. Promise that you aren't going to mention their name or other identifying information to your staff, if they have a problem with a specific person they want to get off their chest.

Finish up the conversation asking if the client has any suggestions for improvement in your salon's services. At this point, hopefully the client will be primed and ready to open up a little more; then you'll get the real answer.

Still, it's possible the client will be too polite or hesitant to give you the real story, despite your efforts to feel it out. Be careful not to let your frustration show, or reveal you're possibly trying to get dirt on a staff member. The client will most likely shut down.

If you can't get the story gracefully, just accept you may never get it at all. Thank the client warmly for their time and express your wish to see them again soon. Simply making the gesture might cause the client to reconsider and give you a second try, just because you're so darn polite!

Although, showing your gratitude with a special offer or coupon for a product or future service wouldn't hurt either. Offer something valuable and tempting. Don't press too hard, but make the offer to mail a coupon, gift card, or voucher as a thank-you gift for their time. They may still be angry enough to say no, but they will probably appreciate your gesture. Best-case scenario, it might just get them back in the door, long enough for you and your staff to prove you're back on your game and ready to play the client's way.

33

Cut Costs or Die!

Today's business owners have so much to do in so little time, it makes the simple things like trimming everyday operational costs a nuisance. The fact is, the smallest costs are the ones that add up without you knowing it. Most salon owners look at their biggest costs and assume rent, payroll, and insurance are their biggest problems, and who can do anything about those? But the real lost opportunity is in overlooking the daily operational costs that can start as a small leak and end up quickly sinking the business.

In good times and bad, it is always a good idea to look at overall business costs, not just the big expenses. Keeping an eye on the bottom line means watching every dime that comes in and goes out of your business daily.

Do something or die is not a phrase I use lightly; it simply highlights the fact that in order to survive, things need to change, but where to start is the question. It's not that hard and doesn't require a ton of effort. Let's open your books and eyes to the most effective and quickest strategies you need to consider in order to cut costs today!

Stop Spending Now—Unless you absolutely need supplies, don't spend a dime on anything. If you need coffee, water, bathroom supplies, cleaning fluids, or whatever else it takes to run your salon, make sure that the purchase is needed and is approved by you, your assistant, director, manager, and partners.

When you *do* allow a purchase, make sure you review the receipt so you know the person buying the supplies is accountable for whatever it is they purchased. If you're doing the buying, spend a few extra minutes to look for discounted items. Cut coupons if it means saving a few bucks. You can't be too proud for coupon-clipping when you're in the "cut costs or die" mode!

Staff Expenses—If you trust your employees to run an errand, or meet with your distributor or make a lunch appointment with your marketing person, and they put in an expense report, you must review all expenses they're claiming. This type of thing shouldn't happen a lot in the salon, but if it has been the policy up until now, stop all staff expenses until you get your business back on its feet. There may be some murmurings or complaints, but impress on your staff the need to cut the perks.

Bank Expenses—Banks today are looking to make more money by charging small businesses fees for all the regulatory changes.

Most businesses are held hostage by all these fees. How many of us don't take time to check our statements to see what we pay monthly in fees? We need to be on our toes and be proactive about avoiding these costs. Here are some of the bank fees you to look out for:

- ATM-use charges
- Bounced check fees
- Check-processing fees
- Debit card fees

If your bank isn't willing to eliminate these fees for doing business with them, eliminate *them* and shop for a new bank that won't charge you for these services. You'll be surprised how fast you can save a couple hundred dollars.

Credit Card Balances—Every one of us gets prescreened credit card offers in the mail almost daily, offering special programs and perks. Ninety-nine percent of the time, we don't even open the mail to see what the offering is.

Okay, it's time to open one of those envelopes and see what the lowest rate is. If you have any credit-card debt on your salon's card, I can guarantee you are paying over 23% interest, maybe even as high as 30%, and that's compounding daily. So, transfer that high credit-card debt onto a card that's offering 0% interest as an introductory offer. If you have multiple credit cards you owe money on, try to consolidate all those balances onto one or two cards with low or no interest.

The interest charges you won't be paying mean you will instantly save some pretty big money the next time your bill is due. You can apply this rescued cash to what you currently owe or use the extra dollars for another bill you wouldn't have been able to pay easily otherwise. Revisit the chapter "How to Use Your Salon's Credit Cards as Life Rings" for more tips.

Note: Interest on credit cards never goes away, it keeps growing daily, weekly, and monthly. The retail you bought two months ago and sold and still haven't paid for will end up costing you a fortune and you're going to lose all the profits you may have thought you made.

Credit-Card Processing—When you started your salon, you may have quickly signed up for a credit card processing company, without much thought. Most business owners don't fully investigate the cost of processing each and every one of their clients' credit cards. It seems like everyone uses plastic and barely even recognize cash anymore. Some don't even carry it. And personal checks? What are those, again? Credit cards and in, in, in, but your tab to process your clients' charges can be quite large. I talked about this issue back in "How to Keep Your Money in Your Wallet and Out of the Drain," so check back for more detail.

A 2% fee is the norm in the industry and that would be a fair rate. If you're paying even a tenth of a percentage point over that, you're paying too much. You can quickly put hundreds, if not thousands of dollars, back into your business by switching and reducing the amount you're being charged to process credit cards.

Plug the tiny leaks and you may just save the entire ship! Re-examining all the small expenses and expenditures can be the difference between a floating boat and a sinking one. Don't expect to avoid bailing a lot of water—some back-breaking work is unavoidable—but at least you'll have hope your efforts can pay off.

34

Market Your Business or Perish!

When you opened the doors of your salon or took over the role of manager, you probably threw yourself immediately into the day-to-day doing of business. You assembled a good team of stylists and now things are going well, but are your struggling to get to the next level, beyond hand-to-mouth business? It might be a stretch to pay the bills and you don't see the bottom-line number growing. New clients flocked through the doors at first, but now they're only trickling in. What's going on here?

In the beginning, you were going to hire a Web designer and build an impressive Web site for your salon, but you never seemed to have the time and money to do it. Fast forward to today and you still haven't done much in regards to advertising the salon.

Why do companies even advertise? Simple: It works. In the technological age, your clients expect to be able to do almost everything from their computer or phone. If your business is not accessable by either, how will potential clients find you? If you don't have online presence these days, you might as well not have physical presence. Gone are the old days of the Yellow Pages. Let's face it, if people can't find you via Google, Yelp, Angie's List, Bing, or whatever, they're going someplace else. I'm sure you've done this yourself; so have I. Why wouldn't your clients?

If you're not online today then how can you expect your business to sustain itself and grow? Advertising online provides your salon with the most cost-effective method to reach the greatest percentage of clients available in your area and beyond.

Example 1: A family of five moves into your community and is looking for a hair salon for their family's needs. They immediately go to the Web to find the salon that's close to home, sells specific grooming products Mom, Dad, and Big Sister use, and offers prices that fit their family budget.

Example 2: A family is flying into town for a wedding and the girls need to have their hair and makeup done for the wedding ceremony and pictures. They need these services in proximity to the wedding hall and the salon needs to be open early.

Example 3: A woman in town had her hair done while on vacation, the stylist did a rotten job, and the woman's hair was damaged badly. She wants to go to a color specialist in town, but doesn't know what salon specializes in damaged hair; she turns to the Web to find out.

So, now are you starting to understand the problem? If you can't be found and they don't know what your salon looks like, where it's located, what services you offer, retail products you use and sell, and what time you open and close, they will go elsewhere for their service. These three examples are only a few business opportunities your salon and staff might be missing on a daily basis.

Out of "Site," Out of Mind

You'll never realize the missed opportunities due to your lack of a Web site, because you'll never see what business you're losing to your competitors. That is, you won't until you actually take the time to create a site, and you witness the bump in business that will result!

You realize now you have to make the time and put aside a small budget to get your salon's online advertising started. Nearly every business is on the internet now and you can take advantage of the internet's many free or low-cost tools. You can enjoy the convenience and ease of buying from or learning more about your business online. You need to give your clients new and old what they want by having a presence online. This should be your first step to marketing your salon.

Where to Begin?

The first thing you need to do is to develop branding for your company. Probably you already have some, in the form of business card design and door signage. Your Web site will be more in-depth and interactive.

Put together a list of what you want clients to know immediately about your salon, the most important attributes of your salon and the team you've put together. Your list should include:

- The name of your salon, location, phone, and email address
- Salon logo and company Web site
- Hours of operation
- What services your salon specializes in
- Full salon menu
- What retail products and color you use and sell
- How many stylists you have on your team
- Educational accomplishments of your team
- Photos of satisfied customers
- Cuts and colors you specialize in

Understand that internet advertising opens up a customer base well outside the local area and it's important to include those potential clients in the campaign as well. Utilize company logos and pictures heavily in your new marketing strategy.

Develop a Branding Strategy

Develop a branding strategy for your salon. If you are ready to brand your salon, you need to have a clear understanding of what developing a brand involves, before you really get started. Your brand development should always follow these major steps:

Identify Your Target Market—What type of clients are you attracting? The success of your company's branding efforts will depend on targeting the clients you want to attract. Trendy graphics and slick layout will show your creativity, but remember, if you're going after a broad client base, you might want to lean toward conservative and user-friendly. You don't want to turn off the mature potential client base. Cater to the tastes of your target audience.

Legalities—Make sure your branding is not similar to or could be construed as a copy of another salon's in your area or neighboring town. Developing your brand is a long-term investment. Register your trademark legally to protect your company name from other salons and, more importantly, to avoid client confusion.

Set Up Your Own Web Site—It isn't that difficult to either set up your own Web site or pay someone to set it up for you. You'll have to register your preferred company domain name on www. godaddy.com or www.shopify.com to secure your name as your domain address. The registration cost can be less than $10 a year. Each of these companies will also develop your Web site and logo for a small fee. All this is done online and does not take more than a few hours, for a fully functioning, customer-friendly site.

Your Web site needs to have easily navigated layouts, be filled with useful and interesting information and be free of junk or unhelpful things. Avoid confusion and anything that will discourage a customer from lingering on your site. This is one time when spending a few extra dollars to pay a professional Web designer can be well worth it and will pay itself back in no time.

Clarify Your Brand Definition—Your brand definition describes what your salon offers—from services to intangibles—why you offer them, how your offerings are better, what unique benefits your clients can expect, and what promise or set of promises you make to all who buy from your salon. Focus on your people, how your team, with their awards and honors, are different and outstanding, since people are the most compelling element of a brand.

Mission Statement/Tagline—What is a mission statement? Why do you need one? A mission statement tells something about who you are, what your business represents, and your reason for being in business. The mission statement should guide the actions of the organization, spell out its goal, and give a context for all decision making.

For example, your mission statement might be: "Creating a new look for you!" if you want to capture a sense of artistic drive and fashion-forwardness. Your mission statement might be: "Making a difference with every cut!" if you want your salon to be a civic-minded organization that donates regularly to community causes.

Develop Your Logo and Color Scheme—Choose simple, complimentary colors and an easy-to-read font for your company logo. Choosing a graphic that says something about your business helps in creating your salon's brand. Probably you want a concrete visual image, maybe of scissors or ringlets or a stylized face, instead of interlocking letters or the like. You're running a salon or spa, not a consulting firm.

Your logo is the symbol that serves as the face of your salon's brand. It needs to somehow reflect your product, brand, and market position. Your logo should be memorable and unique, so your clients can recognize it in the blink of an eye.

Launch Your Brand—Your brand goes public when you unveil your name, new logo, and mission statement online. You now can begin to market your salon on the Web and show how your brand reflects what your salon stands for!

Once you launch your Web site on the internet, you're going to have to advertise in strategic locations to maximize results. Search engines often use keywords or phrases to locate Web sites. Target specific keywords to ensure search engines are drawn to your salon's Web site. Where your company shows up on the search engines is extremely important. The first page is really the only option. If your Web site appears on the second page or thereafter, it's completely ineffective.

Your Web developer can discuss a plan to target advertisements on strategic locations. Once everything is in place, use ads on major Web sites to propel interest in your salon. The ads should drive people back your Web site or social media pages. Google and AdSense are the most popular and can be tailored by location, customer profile, or other search criteria. The nice thing about this advertising method is usually you only have to pay when someone clicks on the link. Money is tight right now, so you may want to utilize pay per click on the slowest days in the salon. This all can be worked out and is very easy to establish.

Remember, there's more to online advertising than putting your Web page on the internet. That being said, it takes a lot of effort to get saturation on the internet. Keep in mind you were invisible up to this point! Celebrate the small victories with your staff and clients along the way to keep you motivated.

YouTube and Your Business—One of the most popular and creative ways to show off you salon business in through YouTube. Seems like everyone has a cellphone that can record videos these days. If you don't, someone surely does in your salon. Take some videos of your staff cutting hair, coloring clients, and showing off your best results.

Record clients while they're getting their hair done and let them talk about how great your salon and staff are. Everyone wants to be the star for a day, so make your clients stars. Post regularly. It's free! I have a motto all salon managers should follow: If it's free, it's for me. Take advantage of YouTube now.

Upload your videos on all sorts of hair and beauty topics, so as many people as possible see it. These links should also be posted on your Web site.

Examples:
- How to fix damaged hair
- How to fix split ends
- How to straighten hair
- How to set curls that will last all day
- How to look beautiful on the fly
- Makeup for a daytime event versus makeup for a night out

Salon Blog—This is one way you can promote your salon without spending any money: You can blog whenever you have free time. I know time is limited—with work and family and everything else—but this advertising is free. Yes, time is money but blogging moves your company up on the search engines organically. Organically, you say? No, this is not about healthy food, it's about healthy advertising. Take advantage by writing about your salon team, products you use, the clients' hair you saved, the client who has cancer you helped by making them look and feel beautiful. All these blog posts will help your clients new, old, and future find your salon on the internet.

Email Marketing—It makes good business sense to be in touch with your customers on a regular basis. You need to have a list of all your customers, or potential customers, you can keep in touch with by email on a regular basis. Send an email about a product launch or a special visit from one of you distributors, featuring a special product. Sending your clients an email thanking them for their past visit is also a nice touch. A quick reminder of an upcoming appointment is also a nice way to say, "Hello, looking forward to seeing you for your next appointment."

Monthly specials or product being featured for Mother's Day or the winter holidays can be sent in bulk email. It shouldn't be that expensive and certainly won't take that much time, once you've programmed it the first time. With a click of a button, all your clients can get a quick hello from you and your salon. How cool is that?

Get on Facebook Now!—If you're not on Facebook, then get on it by the end of today. The whole world connects on Facebook. It's free! Once your salon gets up on Facebook, you and your entire team can have fun posting photos of clients and staff, plus events your salon hosts. Your customers will love being connected with the salon. It's a great way to showcase your salon's talents and what's happening. Make time to post something every day.

Once your salon has a Facebook account, make sure it's optimized so you get the most from it. Use Facebook ads, updates, and a fan page to keep your customers informed about your business offerings and happenings.

You can use your salon's Facebook account to host friendly competitions. How about the worst hair day? Have your clients post pictures; your staff members can start it off with their own photos. Whoever has the worst hair, wins a small prize. Follow up on the competition with a message about how your salon can fix even the worst bad-hair day, so you can tie the competition back to your services. Now that's sweet!

Twitter, Tumblr, Pinterest, Instagram, and All the Rest—It seems like there's a new Web phenomenon every ten days in today's world. It pays to do a little with each one, so you can reach a lot of different kinds of people. Maybe all the young people in town are using Instagram and have jumped off the Facebook bandwagon. Does that mean you should, too? No way. You want your salon's name, logo, and brand definition in front of every pair of eyes possible.

However, you need a strategy. If your clients use two or more social media sites, they don't want to see the same twelve photos on each one; that's boring. Sit down with your Web developer, your salon team, or both and map out which sites you're going to use and which you're going to take a pass on. Maybe you have time for Twitter but Tumblr would be overwhelming. Maybe Tumblr is all the rage with your clients and you have to have a presence there, but your audience is not the StumbleUpon demographic.

Your team members are with-it people and probably know what social media sites are the most popular or suit the needs of the salon. Don't be shy about asking your clients about it, either! If you can, create a survey to ask clients what internet sources of beauty and fashion information they're using the most these days. If a paper survey is too time consuming or just passé, start a conversation about social media while you're trimming or coloring your clients' hair.

Take the pulse of your potential audience, then map out how you're going to use each social media site. Maybe your videos of happy clients go on Facebook but you want your how-to videos of staff, along with a video introducing your salon, on YouTube. Decide what kind of photos go on Twitter and what kind go on Instagram. Get advice from your team, clients, and Web developer on how best to take advantage of all the options out there.

Get Up, Get Online

There are so many way to advertise your company without spending a lot of money. The steps we took in this chapter will set you on the right path. Keep in mind, if haven't used any means of advertising and you focus on the methods in this chapter, you now have taken the first necessary steps to propel your company from the bottom of the ocean into sailing on calm waters. If you don't market online, your business will die. If people can't find you, how do you expect to attract new business? In today's Web-based world, you must be present and easily found with a click of a button or mouse. All this can be done without spending a ton of money and will pay great dividends down the road.

35

The Fine Line Between Marketing and Harassment

Most of us get inundated with emails. If you sign up for a credit card, visit your optometrist, shop online, get your car fixed, go to your hair salon for your routine touch-up, or just visit a Web site for information, everyone wants your email address. Once you give it, what happens next is the onslaught of promotions, sales, gimmicks, gadgets, store events, dating-site advertisements, and, yes, appointment reminders.

Sure, it's easy to delete messages you don't care about, and it's a lot less annoying to get an email advertisement than a call from a real, live telemarketer. Still, it's so aggravating to have to delete a dozen junk emails, or forwards with antique jokes, before you can even settle down to read the note from your mom.

I, for one, can say it's enough work to filter through emails from friends, family, and acquaintances, but at least I know them.

How about everyone else? It seems like it's bordering on harassment that some of these businesses constantly bombard us with email blasts. If I get one more email about a vacation I can't afford, I'm going to throw my computer!

Yes, we can ask to be removed from the email chain or subscription list. Alas, it's not always so simple, especially if you asked to get emails from this company because you genuinely like to buy their product, *sometimes*. The question is: What's the magic number? Where is the dividing line between a necessary, welcome email from a business and another piece of spam? As a salon business, you have to find the balance of good customer service and respecting people's privacy.

The Email Tightrope Walk

Customer service is an important part of owning a successful salon. The benefit of the internet and email marketing is you can stay in touch with your clients and attract new clients, all for a low price, or no cost at all. The possibilities for attentive customer care are endless!

As a salon owner or manager, you know the importance of constant communication with your clients. How easy is it to just email them a reminder about their next hair appointment and also include a query to find out if they're low on hair-care products, or include a plug about a launch sale for a new product?

Yes, all of the above are reasons to send out an email, but how many times do you need to send a good client an email about their next appointment. Once, twice, three times? I guess there's no magic number, but too many emails about the same thing maybe means your clients stop reading your salon's emails altogether, so the benefit is lost. The inexpensive communication tool is gone and your emails end up in the black hole of the spam filter or junk-mail box. Or worse, your client sighs in exasperation at *another* email from you and sweeps them all out of the inbox!

How many times you email is totally up to you and should be based on feedback you get from your clients directly, or the good advice you get from your PR team, Web developer, or marketing person, if you have these resources. The norm in the industry, though, is that two weeks from the appointment, you can start emailing your customer. Two emails should be plenty. If you're having a sale or a special promotion at the salon let them know by emailing them no more than 3 times, starting one month before the event happens, with the final email arriving in their inbox the day before the event.

I've received a bunch of emails from readers (and I read each and every one of them!) lamenting their lack of ideas for types of email communications. My advice? Think about what you would say to your clients if they were standing right in front of you in your salon, or if a client called you on the phone and asked "what's new?" Put that in the email; write it in your own voice.

E-Newsletters

Use an email newsletter to keep in touch with your customers on a regular, scheduled basis and collect all the information they need in one place. Most people would rather have a lot of information in one, central location than a ton of information tidbits in a bunch of different emails.

Your newsletter can include articles on topics of interest to your readers, relevant news, case studies, your own commentary on the issues of your industry, useful information about your products or services, and—my personal favorite—hints and tips.

An e-newsletter can help you:

- Build relationships with your clients and potential clients
- Position you and your company as valuable resources
- Obtain and retain some real estate in your clients' memory
- Educate and inform clients about the world of cosmetology
- Illustrate the advantages of your salon's specific offerings
- Widen your audience through word-of-mouth referrals, if a client clicks "Forward," after seeing an article a friend would like

A newsletter serves as a subtle reminder for clients to return to your Web site, buy your retail products, and, most importantly, visit your salon for services! Remember the benefit of email is staying in touch without being a nuisance. How many times you email a customer is totally up to you. Think about it from a client perspective; how many times do you personally need to be reminded about an appointment, event in town, sale, or new product launch? How many emails is too many for you? The answers to these questions will give you a good idea about how to run your salon's email campaigns successfully.

36

Renegotiate Your Lease or Die!

When opening your salon, didn't you take a space you fell in love with? The location was fantastic, plenty of parking, visibility from the road, and the hottest area in town. This location was everything you dreamed it could be.

Possibly, you had one major problem: The size was just a little too big. The rent cost was way more than you originally intended to pay, but you figured you would grow into the space, hire extra stylists, and things would be easy after a few months. Am I ringing any bells?

Many salon owners around the country have fallen into this trap. Spaces don't fill themselves; cosmetologists are not too easy to find. Well, let me rephrase that: *Good* cosmetologists are not easy to find. The staff to fill those extra styling stations and two back treatments rooms just haven't materialized. You've been pouring your hard-earned dollars into paying the rent, just to keep the salon in business. It seems like the only one making bank on this deal is your landlord!

Month after month, with no end in sight. You now wonder if the salon can survive. You can't believe this has gone on for as long as it has, because now you've depleted your savings and are at the end of your rope. What can you do save your business?

No one enjoys thinking about this scenario, much less living through it. Strangely, though, the economic downturn has helped many business owners in this very situation. With so many businesses closing their doors, there's been an increase in the availability of commercial space. That means many landlords are nervous about losing their tenants.

This gives tenants an unusual amount of leverage to approach the landlord for concessions, which most likely did not exist when first negotiating the lease. If you have no choice but to ask your landlord for a rent reduction, here are the strategies I suggest you use.

Prep Yourself

Step 1: Ask Around—The first step is to contact a local realtor. Have a conversation about commercial availability in your area. Ask what the current rate is for a comparably sized space and if there's any room for tenant improvement. If you have time to visit one or two of the locations that's similar to yours, I suggest you do it.

Once you have an idea about availability and price breakdowns, you can set the stage for a conversation with your landlord. Being educated in what's going on in your area will only help you when trying to negotiate. Going in blind and not knowing the rental climate around your location will lessen the chance of a successful negotiation with your current landlord. The goal here is to show that pricing has changed since you signed your lease and, if something can't be worked out, you'll be forced to move. Trust me, that's the last thing your landlord will want to hear!

Questions to ask the realtor before you call or meet with your current landlord:

- What is the rent in this area?
- How many vacant spaces are in this area?
- What are other landlords doing to attract new tenants?
- Are there any new strip malls or shopping centers in the area?
- How many businesses my size have gone out of business?
- Are any landlords willing to give six months free rent, or some other concession, if I move into their space?
- Could you give me a list of spaces, plus their addresses and market evaluations?

Step 2: Sales Reports—How are your sales? Most business owners don't like to discuss them, never mind show their current financial state to anyone, especially their landlord. But remember, this may be your last go at trying to turn the corner and get your business back on its feet. Have a meeting with your landlord and be an open book. You're basically showing everything to your landlord, holding nothing back, with the hope that he or she knows the economic climate and can truly empathize with the financial state your business is in.

Here are the items to request from your accountant or bookkeeper, before talking with your landlord:

- Last year's sales numbers
- Current sales numbers for this fiscal year
- Current interim statement
- List of all expenses in the salon, including: product purchases, phone bill, internet, insurance, payroll, electric, gas, marketing, bookkeeping, and, most important, rent.

The goal is to negotiate a restructuring of your lease. Having your sales numbers with you will only assist in making your case.

Step 3: Make the Phone Call—The hardest thing to do as a business owner is to call your landlord and explain you're having a tough time surviving and need his or her help. It's a blow to your pride in so many ways. When you dreamed of being a salon manager, none of this crossed your mind. Why would it? You're the best stylist in your area. People love you and can't wait to get back into your styling chair. Still, anyone can bite off more than they can chew, and operating in the slowest economy since the Great Depression can take down the best of businesses, why not yours?

When you call to speak to the landlord, ask to have a business meeting outside of their office and your salon. The last thing you want is distractions from either the landlord's staff or yours. Make the appointment in the morning, when both you and your landlord are fresh and most alert. Schedule no more than an hour. This will certainly be enough time to get the job done. Most likely this will be the first of several meetings, so save it for later.

Strategies for setting the meeting:

- Call the landlord and say you want to discuss the state of your business (don't let the cat out of the bag on the phone)

- Make sure you make the appointment sooner rather than later. Most landlords think they have the upper hand, so they may try to avoid a meeting.
- The longer you wait, the worst shape you will be in financially, so make the call a.s.a.p.

Step 4: The Meeting—This will not be a walk in the park. Asking your landlord for a rent reduction is going to take finesse, and a lot of guts! It's going to be easy for this meeting to turn into a sob story or a mud-slinging fight, so think carefully about your approach. Remember, you aren't spoiling for a fight and accusing your landlord of being a greedy tyrant; you're informing him or her of a way to make the business relationship more profitable for both of you. That's a positive thing!

In the meeting, focus on what the landlord wants: A strong business in their space that makes plenty of money to pay rent on time, attracts a great clientele who will spend money in other spaces the landlord might own in the neighborhood, and increases the value of the property. The landlord wants to say to potential tenants of other spaces, "Salon XYZ is right next door to this space and that's the busiest, most profitable salon in town."

Now, keep the conversation driving toward how your salon fits into the landlord's needs, as you present the challenges facing your business. Talk about how the weak economy is affecting your business specifically. Save the information on competing spaces in the area for later; show your sales and profits first, to demonstrate the needs your business has. Share your plans for how you're going to make your salon more competitive (marketing plan, improvements, costs you're cutting elsewhere, etc.), once you have some cash freed up to do so. Only now can you bring up the reason for the meeting: Your need for lower rent.

Hopefully your landlord will get the picture immediately, but it's possible he or she won't agree to renegotiating your rent right away. He or she might even feel put on the spot and become defensive. Not good for you. Remember to keep your cool, keep your hands on the steering wheel, and drive the conversation back to the positive course of making this business relationship beneficial for both of you.

At this point, you could carefully bring up how the changes in the economy are affecting rent prices in the area. Show your data about the deals other landlords are offering and how it would be a good business tactic to try the same thing. Important! This is not the time for you to be making threats of moving out! Your landlord has probably already figured out that's a possibility. Do you want to do long-term business with someone who uses the so-long-sucker approach? Neither does your landlord, but he or she will more than likely be willing to play ball with someone smart, informed, calm, and fair.

Step 5: Follow Up—No matter the outcome, thank your landlord for taking the time to meet with you. Hopefully, you can also thank him or her for the new deal you just shook hands on! After you leave the meeting, follow up quickly with any documents you need to sign. Also, think about sending a thank-you note to your landlord, just to cement your image as a gracious tenant and a good person to have around.

Win, lose, or draw, it's worth your time and effort renegotiating your lease or rent rate with the landlord. Sure, it's going to be about as much fun as a root canal, but think how much money you could conserve and how that might just be the tipping point for your business. No pain, no gain and you've got a salon to save!

37

Employee Theft Could Sink Your Business

Picture this: you have tried every conceivable attempt to trim expenses and build your salon business, but nothing seems to be working. Day after day, you stand behind your chair and work your buns off. Your clients are happy, your salon stylists are busy, and the chairs are constantly full. Your product distributor tells you your retail sales are the healthiest in the area. Things seem to be okay, but the trouble is, you're barely paying your monthly bills and making payroll. You can't seem to figure out why things aren't getting better. Life is so busy, you need for things to turn around or you could possibly lose your business, home, family, and most importantly, your mind!

Maybe one day, while working with a client, your banker calls and says your business account is overdrawn. You knew things were tight, but not that bad. That evening you look closely at your books and business checking account, something you normally don't do and haven't for a long time. Your longtime friend and bookkeeper did this for you, since you opened the salon. Managing your books was not something you were good at and your friend sold you on her ability to do this for you at a reasonable salary. You figured you could concentrate on what you do best: cut and color and grow your business. What you discover when you sit down with the books, though, is overwhelming.

In this case, an accidental discovery in the accounts reveals that your most trusted, high-level employee and supposed friend has been embezzling money from you since day one of you opening your salon business, unnoticed for years—until now!

Do you think this could never happen at your salon? Think again. Could it be happening now? When is the last time you checked your books, balanced your checkbook, looked closely at receipts, and checked inventory coming and going through the salon? When did you last even peek at your managers' expenses?

Studies have shown people are honest about 80–83% of the time. Sure, that's the majority of people the majority of the time, but what *about* that other 17–20% of the time? Security experts say that as much as 30% of the average company's employees *do* steal, and 60% of the other folks *will* steal if given a motive and opportunity. Remember: Opportunity makes a thief!

Some estimates indicate that more than $600 billion is stolen annually, or roughly $4,500 per employee. According to the U.S. Department of Commerce, about a third of all business failures each year trace back to employee theft and other employee crime.

Given these figures, it's important you protect your salon against theft, and take the proper steps if you discover a thief. Here's how you can do just that.

Become Familiar with the Common Ways Employees Steal

Those who want to steal from you can get very creative, and you must understand how theft happens so you stay one step ahead of them and their schemes. The most common ways employees steal fall into the categories of larceny, skimming, and fraud.

1. Larceny is the actual stealing of property or cash. It's often the easiest to detect because usually the cash or product has already been recorded in the computer system or the books and adequate controls exist. But different ways this can happen include pocketing loose change or stealing goods before they reach the shelves.

   Example: Retail products start to disappear. You think staff may be using the extra retail products on clients, but in fact the thief steals inventory, just enough to go unnoticed, and either sells it to the client and pockets the money or sells the product after they leave the salon each day. A salon employee stealing inventory may drop products in the garbage behind the salon and pick them up when they leave or after the salon is closed, instead of hiding them in their purse or bag.

2. Skimming is embezzling cash before it's even recorded on the company's books. This can happen when an employee has a client pay them directly for products or salon services. Receivables' skimming is when the amount owed is reduced in the computer system or in the books. Over-billing is another method of skimming, when employees with permission to submit business expenses turn in receipts twice and get reimbursed twice or claim more expenses than they actually incurred.

   Example: Your would-be salon thief performs an expensive service for a client. The client goes to pay the bill for service and your employee says the computer is down and asks the client to pay in cash or check, to save time.

3. Fraudulent disbursements. These take several forms, including billing schemes, payroll fraud, register-disbursement schemes, expense-reimbursement anomalies, and check tampering. A stylist or front-desk staff member can charge a client one amount, ring up a bill for less, and pocket the difference. Other schemes include fake payrolls—paying a person who doesn't exist—or purchasing fraud, where employees pretend to buy products for the salon they don't actually purchase, then reimburse themselves. Your employees are suddenly using three times the normal amount of tissues? They don't all have colds; there's theft going on there.

Trust your instincts. When something looks wrong, sounds wonrg, smells wrong, feels wrong, but you can't quite put your finger on it, something probably *is* wrong and it might be theft. Here are some common red flags that the books are cookin' and employees could be stealing:

- Sales of inventory leap, but profits and cash flow are declining
- Products are marked down without permission
- Product sales don't match inventory
- Unclear recording methods, or changes in paperwork or the way your employees handle procedures
- Missing check numbers from the business checkbook
- Unexplained expenses
- Employees padding time sheets
- Payments to suppliers you don't know
- Higher vendor prices you didn't receive notice about
- An increase in bounced checks in your business account

- Unusual or unauthorized salon expenses, such as cleaning, painting, light bulbs, or supplies

Prevent Crime Before It Happens

Since stealing can cost your company a lot of money, the best way to avoid employee theft is to take steps to prevent it from ever happening. While the steps I'm recommending aren't foolproof, they can offer a measure of protection against employees raiding the register.

1. Perform background checks on applicants. Make sure you contact previous employers, references, and schools to look for signs of any misconduct, in terms of stealing or fraud. Consider getting a police report on the applicant. This all takes time, effort, and cash, but it's all well spent. Most of us in the salon business are inclined to trust everyone we meet, but this extra step can save you tons of money in the long run. It may even save your business.

2. Consider giving an "honesty test." These are standardized, commercially available written tests that provide psychological evaluations of an applicant, or even a current employee. While a lot of people believe these tests help keep out potential thieves, there's a risk you have to factor into the equation: Some people think these tests are inaccurate and could violate privacy and civil rights.

3. Supervise your employees. Research has shown that businesses with low levels of employee supervision show high rates of employee theft. You don't have to be a hovering helicopter-mom to all your employees, but do keep your eye out for the telltale signs of theft, such as a rise in an employee's spending

What to Do When Things Are Going Wrong

234

habits. You know how much your employees are supposed to be making, so a Louis Vuitton handbag purchased on a off-brand budget could be a red flag.

4. Make it hard to steal. Don't allow just one person to deal with money. Show up at unusual times to conduct inspections or audits of inventory and the daily reports. Monitor bookkeeping records carefully.

5. Make a fraud-avoidance plan and set the rules. Every business needs to develop a fraud-avoidance and assessment plan and set the rules for consequences if an employee is caught embezzling money from the company. Proper planning will help make certain all employees know where the salon stands in regards to employee theft, and will give you confidence to handle employee theft properly, should it occur. A plan should include: background checks, periodic changing of computer passwords, internal and external auditors, and clearly stated and written consequences of theft. Let people know what's going to happen if you catch them stealing.

Why Employees Steal

Fraud often starts small, then gets bigger and bigger as the fraudster gets bolder. Typically, three factors must be present before an employee commits fraud or embezzles from your salon business: Opportunity, motivation, and rationalization. Let's look at signs you might notice in your employees and salon environment.

Opportunity—In the salon business, it's not uncommon for the owners to put trust in more than one person to help assist with bookkeeping, banking, and the management of the salon business. Life is busy with raising children, managing a home, and, of course, running your business. As salon owners, we are naturally talented in the art of hair, nails, and skin care; we are creative geniuses with making people look beautiful. Unfortunately, many of us lack business management skills. This unfortunate circumstance leaves us vulnerable to would-be thieves.

Usually weak or loosey-goosey—or should I say non-existent?—controls lead to a breakdown in the organizations processes and provide the opportunity for employees to take advantage of you. Again, typically the most trusted people in your salon are the ones who have the opportunity to steal. Remember, trust is a feeling, not a control.

Motivation—The salon industry attracts people from all walks of life. Without background checks or serious due diligence, we can unknowingly hire someone who may have a drug problem, who has been arrested for who-knows-what, who has a gambling addiction, or who just has serious money-management problems. These people are more likely to steal from you. It is so important to screen applicants and perform background and credit checks. Credit checks will show you a wealth of crucial information about your current or future employee.

Background checks and personal credit checks will show:

- Prior addresses
- Prior employment
- All outstanding loans, including mortgages, car loans, student loans, and any others
- All outstanding credit card balances
- If this person has had tax liens
- If the person is behind on child support

- Judgments and liens from employers (very important)
- Names used on their accountants
- Unexplained name changes that might point to fake name use
- If the person has been in jail

This information has to be disclosed on their personal credit report and should be used, once you have permission from the candidate to collect this information, in deciding whether you do or do not hire them.

Rationalization–Some employees just feel they're owed something. They think they're better than the owner or manager or other salon employees, work longer hours, are more creative and much more talented in their hair cutting and coloring capabilities, and therefore are entitled to more. These employees, in their peculiar way of processing values, think they can justify illegal acts of stealing or embezzling from their employer.

This type of employee probably feels grossly underpaid or unappreciated. If they feel like they're doing all the work and the owner is keeping all the profits, why not help themselves by taking what seems rightfully theirs? They feel this is a way to even the score. Another example of rationalization employees use is: "I can borrow a few bucks or some inventory and eventually pay it back." It starts small, they get away with it, the situation snowballs, and it quickly becomes a major problem for you, and for them, too.

Protect Your Business

As business owners and managers, we work so hard to build our business and keep it healthy. The list of daily "to-dos" is a mile long, but watching the cash register and inventory has to be at the top of the list. The best defense is always a good offense.

However, be extremely careful about making accusations before conducting an investigation—a false accusation can bring a lawsuit down on your head, which could kill your business, too. Seek help and legal council if you think you're facing theft, since a legal professional can tell you if you have enough supporting evidence to make a case, and can advise on how to proceed.

Remember these important facts from experienced business owners who have suffered through stealing and embezzling. These are life lessons of the salon business:

- The opportunity to steal is a bigger issue than the money taken.
- Most employees won't tell the owner someone else is stealing.
- Nearly every business has employee theft.
- Nearly one third of business bankruptcies can be traced back to employee theft.

I know these facts are disheartening and give you another reason to wonder why you ventured into salon ownership or management, but employee theft is real and if your business is suffering, you need to open your eyes and see if you can catch a thief!

38

Pull Yourself Out of a Professional Rut

Life is full of repetitive activities, which are there for a good reason. You'd quickly starve to death if you didn't make a habit of eating, right? That's the most basic example, but the necessity of routines travels all the way up the heirarchy of needs. If you didn't pay your bills the same day each month, you would forget them and probably fail to pay. If you didn't see your friends and family regularly, you would feel alone and unhappy. Routines are fine, in and of themselves, but too much of a good thing is no good at all.

We build habits around work and home life, to keep everything in balance and make sure all the necessary tasks get done. You use the same route to work every day because you know it's the quickest. You open the salon on time because the clients and staff expect it. You cut your clients' hair just the way they want it, over and over, even if those clients would look better with something drastically different and exciting. Even in an industry as creative and fun as cosmetology, even owning or managing your own salon and calling the shots, you can find yourself falling into a rut, a funk that sucks the joy out of what you thought you wanted to do with your life. It can be depressing or downright scary.

Getting your butt out of a rut is not easy, especially when you're watching your business flounder along with you. Money is not coming in and things are so tight that you feel guilty stopping at Starbucks for your morning cup of joe, no matter how badly you need it. You feel yourself slipping so far down the rutted trail, you can't find a reason to climb out.

The worst part about being in a rut is your family, friends, staff, and clients can see you're not quite yourself. Being in a rut is contagious and the people you need around you—more than ever!—aren't going to want to be part of it. Remember, clients come to your salon to feel good and leave looking good; your staff looks to you to mentor them. Your usual, fun-loving, Chatty Cathy self seems to have vanished, and if it doesn't come back, you'll quickly run your staff and clients out of town. That town being your salon. On top of being in a personal rut, you don't need a walkout! Hello, you wonder why you're losing customers?

What *is* the way out? How do you get back on top of your game if you don't have motivation in the first place? The best way to get out is to head in a new direction, but in baby steps. You may have the urge to do something drastic and earth-shaking, but before you sell the place, pack up, and move to Australia, try a few simpler and more prudent tactics. Nothing against Australia, I've heard it's amazing, but you've got a business to run.

I'm going to walk you through the necessary steps, starting

with what may seem like baby steps, until you're leaping up the ladder again, feeling like a million bucks and ready to earn that much as well!

Admit You're in a Rut—Coming home from work every day and just falling asleep in front of the TV or computer is good indicator you're in a rut. Tell yourself out loud it's time for a change and it's up to you to do something!

Locate the Source—Look at different areas of your life and try to tease out what area is dragging you down and making you depressed. Work? Social life? Finances? Romance? Can you make a change? Maybe that area, that job, that soulmate, was good in the past, but not anymore.

List Out What Makes You Unhappy—Write down all the things that make you unhappy or depressed, from the worst item in stock all the way up to the smallest offender. Even though the little pet peeve on the list may seem ridiculous, that may be the one that puts you over the top in the first place.

Get Rid of the Stuff!—Once you have identified "the stuff" that's immobilizing you, get rid of it! Like she said in *Frozen*: Let it go. The quicker you do this, the faster you'll start getting your life back on track.

List Out Happy, Inspirational Things—What are you grateful for? Write down all the things that make you happy and put a smile on your face. What do you enjoy doing? Maybe it's going to the gym, cooking, cutting hair, inspiring people, teaching, or simply taking brisk walks outside. Here's a simple but powerful formula:

Happiness=motivation. The simplest things that make you happy are sometimes the most important things. You may have forgotten about these gems or just stopped doing them because of time restraints. Lack of self-care and happiness may be the reason you fell into the rut in the first place.

Disrupt the Normal Routine—Once you have worked out the complexities of your current rut, you will need to break up your normal routine and temporarily change your surroundings. Find a place where you can reflect and plan on making your changes, anywhere that's quiet where you can escape your everyday routine.

Visualize the Goal Line—Review your current situation and evaluate what's going on in your life, of course, but the most important thing is to visualize your destination. What would make you happy? Visualize an image that evokes that goal and hold it in your mind. Keep it simple and don't overdo it. Choose something reachable.

Create a Plan—Create your exit strategy and begin immediately. Don't wait to begin tomorrow or next week. Start right now. Put this book down for a minute, get up, and make a change!

Spring Into Action—When you get up in the morning, think about what you accomplished yesterday and what you are going to do today. Try thinking about what little things you can do that make you happy. What tiny details in life make you feel fulfilled? When you answer these questions, you'll begin to uncover things that inspire you, then you can brainstorm ways to incorporate more of these things into your life.

A tiny, quick change can give you a quick mental fix. Take a break from the salon and your clients by taking a walk around the block. Try a new coffee shop. Try a new product you don't normally use on your own hair. Change your makeup to make you look and feel younger. Whatever it is, don't wait or procrastinate. Life's too short to be sitting in a rut.

Don't Try to Be Perfect—If you're in a rut, the last thing you need to do is pick on yourself for not looking or being perfect. Try to look your best, but hey, if you're having a bad hair day, so what? If the dinner you made your family isn't gourmet tonight, who cares? They're family; they'll understand Do what you can, at your own pace. Let yourself make mistakes. You've heard it before, now you're hearing it from me: Don't sweat the small stuff.

Exercise—When we're stuck in a rut, the first thing to go out the window is health and personal care. In fact, often that's the first sign people around you will notice: You don't look healthy; you might even look downright sick. Starting to feel good about yourself may not only mean working on your brain, but also your body.

Joining a gym or a running club will put you on track for a healthier and better life. Exercise produces natural endorphins; take advantage of a guilt-free high as you go for a jog, lift some weights, or even just power-walk around the park. As you improve your physical health, your mental health will improve, too, because all our facets are interconnected.

Eat and Drink Right—Eating a healthier diet and keeping yourself hydrated will also get your engine running, driving you out of your rut. The Institute of Medicine recommends men drink thirteen 8-oz. glasses of water a day and women drink nine. Are you even close to that? Also, consider cutting your sugar intake down or out entirely. Sugar can provide rushes and crashes that aren't healthy, especially when your emotional health is unstable. Back away from the soda.

Soundtrack—Turn off the Adele and turn on the Beyoncé! If you're depressed and stuck, listening to sad music will not help you one bit. You may identify with it, it may sound exactly how you feel (sad), but you're reading this list because you want to change that. Make a playlist that makes you want to dance and sing, then take it everywhere with you! Play your upbeat music at work. That'll get your energy going! Music affects us on such a deep level; use it.

Muster Your Willpower—Willingness to change is the most important step in making changes in your life; it trumps everything else. No will, no change!

Express Gratitude—Gratitude is an extremely powerful force. It boosts your energy levels, puts you in a positive frame of mind, and makes what you want in life rush toward you! Regardless of your current income, present physical health, or success at work or in your relationships, you have a thousand reasons to be thankful. Let go of self-pity. It's part of your rut, so let it drop. When you focus on what's important in life and express gratitude daily for all that you have, you draw positive energy and opportunity toward yourself.

Call for Help—Rome wasn't built in a day and fixing the business problems in your salon and your personal life will not happen overnight. If you feel like you're slipping down into quicksand, call for help. Call your mentor, accountant, attorney, life coach, business coach, or, last resort, a shrink. Just tell them your problems; talking about it will help. Ask them for advice. Ask them to help you overcome this slump. It works. Just having people hear you out and empathize is healing. Who knows? You may get just the pep talk you need.

The Rainbow Is Coming—One problem you'll face on your way out of your rut is the tendency to think how hard your problems are to fix. OMG, can I do it? Negative thoughts can bring down the strongest person, just like the wind can bring down a the tallest tree. Don't think about how hard something is, but what will come out of it. I call this the rainbow effect. Don't look at how big the mountain you have to climb is, but how big the rainbow will be, once you get to the top! Your perspective on things will look brighter if you visualize a positive outcome.

Evolution Is Good

Life is all about change; there's no escaping it. Change is good and the person willing to accept change will be the happiest. Nothing in the universe is stationary; not the ocean, not the earth, not the galaxy. We are in either in a process of growth or in a process of decay. Look at what happens to fruit just as it reaches its ripest stage—it reaches the peak of sweetness, but then it rots.

Success and happiness are not a destination to be reached. To find both, you must keep traveling on a continuing journey and maintain an attitude of gratitude, no matter your current circumstances. Along the journey, you'll experience change and a lot of it will be good, so don't be afraid of it.

An inspired individual rises each day enthusiastically, ready to face the day head on, knowing challenges and obstacles are nothing more than speed bumps along the road to success, wealth, and fulfillment. Work on what you love and what makes you happy. Seize opportunities; eat the fruit while it's fresh and sweet.

Be inspired at your profession; you've chosen a great one. Be happy and grateful for what you have today. Work on being the best you can be with friends and family. Inspire others and mentor anyone who's willing to listen!

On this journey, you have to look at what makes you happy. Doing something because you love it, instead of for the money, is a powerful beam to send into the universe. Your passion will surely inspire you and make you feel good about your life and future. Tap into that! The money will come, if you consistently act out of inspiration.

21873377R00147

Printed in Great Britain
by Amazon